COMMENTS from READERS

"Truly a book for healing depression.
I needed a spiritual guide, and it lifted
me up – like having a friend with me."

"We took turns reading this book
to each other.
Much the best way to enjoy it –
shared aloud with close friends.

"At last I have a name for
the God of My Understanding."

"It reminded me that I'm proud
to be a crone, myself."

"I repeat the 'credo for women'
every morning when I get up. What an
affirmation! It's changed my life!"

"A meditation in the manner of St. Ignatius."

"Where can I go for those workshops?"

OTHER BOOKS by the AUTHOR

"... and a PEACOCK on the PORCH"
By Mira Leighton

"DETACHMENT"

"ENABLING"

Two small books by
Rebecca D. Chaitin, and
Judith M. Knowlton

"LISTEN to the ACTION"

"TWELVE CHRISTMAS GIFTS"

Both by Judith M. Knowlton

CRONE;

A MEDITATION On WOMANHOOD

By
MIRA LEIGHTON

Originally edited by
Rebecca D. Chaitin

QUOTIDIAN PUBLISHERS
CUSHING, MAINE

2009

CRONE; A Meditation on Womanhood

Copies may be purchased through
www.amazon.com

QUOTIDIAN PUBLISHERS
377 River Road
Cushing, Maine 04563
Judydownmaine@roadrunner.com

CRONE; A Meditation on Womanhood

ℂONTENTS

CRONE; A Meditation on Womanhood

EDICATED

To the joyful memory of my grandmother

BERTHA LEIGHTON JACKSON

Who bestowed on me unconditional love,
Revealed the pleasures of sweet fern,
the fairy accessories in a bleeding heart flower, and
shared the secret of the whippoorwill's call.
Well into her nineties, she still wrote coherent
weekly letters to friends and relatives.
"I am content," she once told me,
"just to live each day as it comes."

CRONE; A Meditation on Womanhood

CRONE; A Meditation on Womanhood

$\mathcal{W}$ELCOME

$\mathcal{C}$HAPTER ONE

"What am I doing, in the midst of a mountain meadow, heaven knows where...?" Augusta was thinking, as she balanced precariously on a water-weather-smooth rock, the toes of her moccasined feet gripping the stone, heels sliding blindly to find a level surface.

A muscle spasm shot along the sole of her right foot and threw her forward. Her eyes darted from stone to rock to bare-bleached tree stump in the dry creek bed, trying to find a place to step. She gripped her walking stick, desperation sweeping across her face, and at last the stick jammed between two rocks, slowing her descent. The effort sprayed perspiration along her upper lip and tickled it along the creases under her heavy breasts. What an obscene feeling, she mused idly, but at least they're not yet withered. And who was it in literature had those withered breasts? Her thoughts drifted on, as she slid slowly and heavily onto the round, sun-warm rock, bruising her thigh.

"A lot worse places to die, Augusta," she continued more comfortably, now that she was seated, "withered breasts or no." She had recently given herself permission to talk out loud to herself whenever the mood came over her, consent having become necessary because she was doing it so often anyway. "Comforting and companionable," she had explained it, liking the alliterative sounds – and recalling how silly and even embarrassing her own grandmother had seemed, as she stood at the fruit stand muttering, "Not quite ripe," and "Let's look at this one again," to herself, all the while sniffing melons, or stealthily testing the tough skin of an orange with her fingernail. The memory instantly evoked the sharp, bittersweet fragrance of orange rind. And was Augusta fast becoming a silly old woman as well? It was perversely satisfying to think she was carrying on a laughable and yet somehow meaningful tradition.

What insane decision had catapulted her into this lonely place? The true purpose of the journey hadn't yet been revealed to her. Today she had simply awakened, as if from an alcoholic's nightmarish blackout, and was compelled to follow this country path. Without written directions, or so much as a map to tuck into her leather backpack, she continued her thought, imagining this to be some medieval quest. Where was she going? The "instructions" that came to mind had been simple enough: a path, a cottage, and a message: "Go toward the sunset." Some vague admonition not to look back, Or had the warning been more specific? Do not try to go back ... one can never go back. Every moment, it was becoming more difficult, as well as less important, to remember the details.

The sun was delightfully warm on her shoulders, and the sky was the sharp, deep blue of high mountains and low humidity. In no time, her natural enthusiasm and sense of adventure had returned, along with the knowledge that her journey was nearing its end. "Augusta, Augusta," she congratulated herself. "The cottage is just over that little rise. I can feel its presence."

Feel its presence? In her younger years, she surely would have brushed off such intuition as magical poppycock. No longer. This older Augusta accepted such "knowings" without question, and acted happily upon them. Life's astonishing twists now filled her with delight instead of fear, even as her family observed that her decisions seemed to be based more on whim than substance.

After all, insecurity was common-place, was life, was truth; wasn't it? How else to explain her easy acceptance of today's curious and unfathomable adventure – not even a little concerned for health or safety?

Gripping her birch staff with both hands, brushing a lock of salt-and-pepper hair from her eye with one shoulder, pulling down her denim skirt, Augusta tried to get up. Her legs were as heavy and flaccid as half-filled sandbags, and she was obliged to roll onto her tender leg and push herself away from the rock with both palms. For the moment, the hiking staff became a real hindrance. She laughed at her awkward situation, surprised once again that her body no longer did her bidding instantly and mindlessly. "Sixty-three is an absurd age," she thought for the umpteenth time, "yet I've the mind and dreams of a twenty year old still – well, but not exactly the *same* dreams," she wryly corrected herself, "nor yet the memory," she hastily amended.

After Augusta had crossed the dry creek bed, the narrow footpath greeted her again, beckoning her forward. She followed its course with her eye, noting how gracefully it skirted rocks and bushes, as it meandered toward the crest of the hill. Her mind took long-legged, loose strides through the field of softly bobbing timothy grass, walking stick swinging in rhythm with her feet, but her travel-tired body resisted the imagery. Only a little frustrated, she gave in to its sedate demands and began slowly to climb.

"Help! Help! Help!" The screams of a terrified woman shattered the gentle early summer air. Adrenaline slammed through Augusta; he heart pounded into her throat. To help or to hide? For a moment she was paralyzed with indecision as her mind manufactured a myriad horrors – a child in danger, a fire raging, a rape in progress ...

From farther off came more screaming pleas, not so loud but just as insistent, the nearer screams playing counterpoint, until the two voices caught up with one another, shrieking now with mounting urgency and in unison, "Help! Help! HELP!"

Augusta leaned on her staff, suddenly flooded with anticipation reminiscent of childhood Christmas mornings – that last quivering moment before one throws off the bedcovers to race to the treasures under the tree. She recognized the creators of those strident screams. Their cries symbolized all the happily-ever-afters that she'd been spoon-fed and eagerly believed as a young girl. She laughed aloud, for surely these were the voices of peacocks.

Inhaling a deep breath of mountain-clean air, the matronly woman stepped forth along the path with a lighter tread, never doubting that the peacocks' screams were the trumpets' flourish, announcing that the curtain was rapidly being raised on today's adventure – the only adventure there is – and the action had already begun.

CHAPTER TWO

Augusta slowed her pace to savor the beauty of the morning, and her anticipation of the surprise over the next hill. It was late June, the countryside clad in the juicy greens of the season, trees appearing freshly washed and polished. A turkey vulture swung lazily overhead, lying effortlessly on the updrafts of the mountain breeze, while several birds sang short, musical phrases from the protective branches of the trees. Beyond the next hill, she could just make out the white church spire in the village of Miraton.

She paused to survey the object of her compelling journey: a small punchbowl valley was laid out before her, shielded from excessive wind and weather. Directly below, a shallow pond glinting in the sunlight commanded the very center of this land basin. The footpath Augusta was traveling aimed straight toward it, then snaked past the water's edge and over a two-plank footbridge that spanned the pond's feeder creek, through a clump of sweet-fern and pines to the doorstep of a two-story stone cottage with a gray slate roof, and a chimney at either end.

This rugged little dwelling was built into the side of a hill, flanked by a matching stone spring-house below it to the right, and a well-tended vegetable garden up the hill a bit to the left – a homestead so trite in its serene beauty and tiny perfection that it was almost laughable. Augusta felt herself brimming over with a heady euphoria, unable to shake the impression that she had designed the place herself, every window and tree placed just so, to her taste and bidding.

She was mesmerized by the creatures scattered about this peaceable kingdom. A gaggle of multi-spotted geese rested near the far edge of the pond. A patriarchal peacock was poised upon the edge of one chimney, where its exotic blue neck and tail-feathers seemed not at all gaudy or out of place. Several reddish-bronze chickens pecked in the dirt before the cottage door, while their rooster, perched on the wide windowsill, quietly enjoyed the warmth of the sun. In the far distance was a miniature barn; near it, a horse and colt grazed comfortably in a fenced pasture. Farther still, a deer-feeder trough lingered at the edge of the woods.

"Idyllic," thought Augusta, "Ineffably idyllic." She smiled at her own pompous but accurate words and inhaled deeply, as if sucking that one last breath before plunging into an icy pool. Swinging her staff forward, she strode deliberately down the sloping path toward the old stone house.

One of the larger geese caught sight of the stranger and lunged to his webbed feet, sounding the alarm. The full gaggle chimed in, squawking and criticizing as they hurriedly splashed into the safety of the water. Augusta laid a foot on the plank bridge, her wooden staff thumping more loudly than she had expected, encouraging the geese to renew their clamor. The hollow sound was like the dampened ringing of a timber bell. The gray-haired woman understood immediately that traversing this span was symbolic, and the wooden knell punctuated its importance. She turned instinctively to look back along the footpath. What was she leaving? What was she forgetting? Startled, she heard the pine trees whisper, "You can never go back." But their muted voices were not ominous. Indeed, they sounded more cheerful than otherwise – as if whispering a blessing.

"I knew that already," she answered aloud, as she peered into the trees dark shadows, and shrugged off the touch of melancholy that had settled for the tiniest minute into her heart.

"What did you know?" The question came gently from somewhere behind her, in an old voice, paper-whisper-thin, yet astonishingly self-assured.

Augusta turned to greet the Crone, never doubting it was she, and found herself gazing into the clear eyes of a woman who was …. and here Augusta began to describe this ancient one to herself in exotic-cosmic terms: "who was as stately-majestic as a flowering tulip-tree, but at once as twisted and gnarled as an unpruned grapevine. Draped in a formless black gown of some changeable weave that caught the color of the peacock and the sunset in its folds – or was it belted, tight-fitting, and black-forest green? She was painfully thin and sinewy, or perhaps she carried the extra weight of a loving-soft, welcoming nanny. And she smelled of …"

"Sweet fern," the Crone completed her thought.

Augusta was startled from her reverie. The old woman had picked a frond from a nearby bush, and was methodically pressing it into her palm with her thumb. The piquant mountain perfume enveloped the two women with its sweetish-wild fragrance, and, in that moment, Augusta recalled her grandmother's reverence for simple things, and thought she knew something about the Crone as well.

"I can never go back," she answered the old woman's question at last. The Crone barely nodded, as if the remark was too obvious to need further consideration.

"Have you come to do for me?" She asked the question in a way that let Augusta know that she had not been looking for anyone.

CRONE; A Meditation on Womanhood

"*Do* for you? Why, I hardly ever 'do' for *myself!*" The younger woman answered with equal parts of honesty and surprise, wondering if the Crone was either touched in the head or senile.

"That's all right, then," the ancient woman responded cryptically. "Come along." And the visitor found herself, perplexed but compliant, on the upward slope of the path leading toward the cottage, wondering why this old woman seemed so very comfortable and familiar, and whether she was ever lonely out here under the mountain.

The Crone walked very slowly indeed, placing her feet with the extreme care of the very old, which allowed the (relatively) younger woman time to look about her. Some of the geese had remained in the pond and were happily, she supposed, standing on their heads to bottom-feed. An enormous, long-haired orange cat with a fat plume of a tail, sprawled on one of the two benches flanking the cottage door, hardly flicked an ear when a scraggly brown puppy tripped over the doorsill, hell-bent on bowling over the Crone. Augusta leaned down to catch the racing ball of energy in her arms, halting abruptly when she realized he was wetting everything in sight. Laughter rose in her throat, echoed by the cough-like cackle of the Crone. Their eyes met for an instant, acknowledging that the puppy's antics gave both of them a moment of perfect pleasure.

"Oh, how adorable!" Augusta exclaimed, as she bent to ruffle the puppy's ears with both her hands. "What's her name?"

The Crone scrutinized the bouncing beast for a moment before answering. "Grumpkin."

Why on earth had such a happy pup been saddled with such a gloomy name? But Augusta didn't want to deflect the old woman from their immediate goal. She was impatient to see the inside of the little cottage. Houses had been a passion throughout her whole life, although she had never fully comprehended the meaning behind the obsession. She only knew that she loved to wander through them, to feel their emotional energy, to visualize how the rooms opened one upon another, to discover the nook where the owner felt most secure and, in her mind, to redecorate the living quarters to her own taste. Sometimes she recognized a primordial need, but at other times she knew it was merely a matter of curiosity -- and control.

"This is Keekah." The Crone extended her hand with the barest movement toward the long-haired orange cat sprawled on the bench. Augusta stroked the lionish animal with rising impatience, though she herself was a true cat-fanatic and had expected to be formally introduced. But at last the old woman gestured for her guest to precede her, and Augusta stepped eagerly over the threshold of the stone cottage, noticing with delight the palpable feeling of contentment emanating from the room, wrapping itself about her.

The first architectural detail she noticed was directly in front of her: a flight of narrow, tread-worn stairs against the left wall, leading steeply upstairs. A plain-hinged door, three boards and a latch, could be closed against the draft from the second floor, retaining the warmth of the fire on the first level. Nestled under the stairs was a tiny wood clothes closet. She turned her gaze to the dim-lit keeping room, and in that moment Augusta knew, with the kind of knowledge born of abiding truth, that this was the very essence of *home*, although the room had few amenities; in fact, it was small, barely furnished, and singularly unadorned.

Two deeply recessed windows, with sills broad enough to curl up in (yes, if you're agile enough, she said with silent sarcasm) opened to a view of the pond behind her; the third window held a view of the springhouse. Rough-spun linen curtains were neatly drawn to one side with a piece of buff-colored twine. The windowless wall, opposite the door, was buried into the hill; the fourth supported a pantry cabinet of age-darkened wood. The walls were white plaster and pictureless. From the ceiling's dark beams hung braids of onions, bunches of lavender, and some herbs Augusta couldn't begin to identify. A narrow fireplace, tall enough for a child to stand in, supported an iron crane with a blackened pot on a hook. It seemed to be the only means of cooking, although a little later she discovered a tiny coal cook-stove, almost out of sight behind the stairs.

CRONE; A Meditation on Womanhood

Two wingchairs flanked the fireplace -- one already commandeered by an extraordinarily fat "Tuxedo" cat lying belly up on the seat cushion. The Crone introduced him to her guest by the curious name of "Sneer," although he didn't deign to make her acquaintance at that moment. A very pregnant white cat, Miss Priss by name, was washing herself contentedly by the fireplace.

This small, spare room contained everything necessary for simple living. A scrub-top oak table and two armless, high-back chairs, were situated between the front windows, presenting a fine mealtime view. A kerosene lamp sat on one windowsill. A small pine cupboard was home to a few mismatched dishes and mugs; a swaybacked shelf of crocks and bottles hung from the wall. To the right of the fireplace stood a zinc-lined sink, with a chipped, green painted hand-pump for drawing water from the well. Augusta shuddered at the thought of washing in such cold water. An enamel pot rested beside the sink, on a dirt floor that was packed to a hard shine from years of use and sweeping. The little room had no rug, no civilizing touches of art or ceramics, except for the gay bouquet of spring meadow grasses and flowers that graced the table. And yet, it was enough. The room felt genuinely loved. Augusta corrected her thought: unconditionally loved.

"Hungry?" the crone asked hospitably, and the younger woman nodded, intrigued and vaguely uneasy about the kind of food that might come forth from such a kitchen.

Soon, behind the stair, came the sound of chopping and stirring. "Bowls," the ancient one commented conversationally from around the corner, and Augusta hastened to the cupboard, with the odd feeling that she'd performed this act untold times before.

The Crone served a ladleful of pungent cream-colored porridge into each bowl from a spotted-enamel, wire-handled bucket. "Potato soup," she explained. But it was far more than that, Augusta thought, for it was a delicate melding of new carrots and mushrooms, onions and basil, with fresh snippets of green chive floating on the surface. And hearty. Beans and rice were hidden within. The two women faced each other across the meadow flowers, bowed their heads for a moment of thanks, and began to eat silently, companionably -- not at all like strangers.

The younger woman – who felt at once like an honored guest and an old friend – was anxious to ask many questions, but thought it might be more courteous to wait for the older woman to open the conversation. Eventually she did.

"Staying long?"

Augusta was surprised. Weren't there a few bits of information to get out of the way first, like names and weather, and living locations? But none of that truly seemed to matter to either of them. "I don't know," she replied. "How long will you have me?"

"You'll know," the Crone answered decisively, as she carried the empty bowls to the sink. And so it was settled. The new houseguest accepted the peculiar arrangement and equally odd relationship without protest. "Your name, my dear?"

"Augusta," the middle-aged woman answered. "I was born in August."

"Hmmm. 'Stately, revered, admired...' Yes, it suits you," the old woman declared with a sharp nod.

Her guest waited patiently for the older woman to introduce herself in return, but she seemed preoccupied, staring off into the distance as if remembering some far-removed time and place. At long last she commented, "I had a name once, before I was myself."

Augusta realized with sharp surprise that the subject was closed abruptly. She *had* a name? Good God, the old woman must indeed be senile. The younger woman felt herself wavering for the first time, questioning her too-easy acceptance of these bizarre circumstances. On a foolish whim she had committed herself to Madam No-Name! Surely it was time to back out – gracefully. Besides, there were some practical considerations here: how was she to address her eccentric hostess? "Crone" was surely insulting and unacceptable, though it reappeared unbidden to her mind. Then too, she wondered why the cottage contained no signs of other peoples' presence – no dim photograph, or carefully chosen gift to acknowledge a relationship. And yet, there was order and discipline here. It was strange. Was the Crone an isolated madwoman whom everyone in town avoided? Nevertheless, as Augusta mulled over these puzzlements, she found herself once again in harmony with the lady of the stone cottage (indeed, why *would* this ancient one require a name like ordinary people), and in tune with the unknown course of her venture.

"Let's go up," the Crone suggested, gesturing with both hands for her houseguest to mount the stairs ahead of her. Drawn out of her musings, Augusta proceeded as she was bidden, noting idly that the staircase creaked very little, considering the obvious age of the house.

On reaching the second floor, she peered through another deep-silled window, glimpsing an outhouse in the woods behind a broad clump of white birches, and said silent thanks for warm weather and clear skies. Her hair brushed the clothes hanging from a Shaker pegboard at the top of the stairs; two coarse wool shawls validated her musing; no doubt they were provided for those shivering midnight sojourns!

Grumpkin had begun to cry from the bottom of the stairs, her voice a sharp yip followed by a lengthy, complaining growl that aptly illustrated the reason for her christening. By the time Augusta had reached the Dutch door on the back wall (where the second floor became ground level), and peered through the open upper half, the puppy was outside, looking up at her hopefully, pleadingly, panting as she wagged her long tail. The Crone, who had taken some time to maneuver the stairs, held up a restraining hand, and shook her head to discourage Augusta from letting Grumpkin through the door.

At the front of the room, two windows opened to a panoramic view of the pond. Two single rope beds, mounded with goose-down mattresses, stood between the windows, and between them, a bedside table held both a kerosene lamp and a candlestick with a glass chimney -- for those late-night travels out back. In addition, two china chamber pots with lids (Augusta's father had called them 'thunder-mugs") were neatly set under each bed, to serve during inclement weather. Similar but unmatched quilts of small pastel squares covered the feather beds, and a ratty rag rug of some nondescript color lay on the wide floorboards between them,

Still another orange cat, looking remarkably leonine, was curled tightly asleep on the single ladder-back rocker. The Crone stroked him gently, pronouncing him to be "Vincent."

The wall against the stairwell was bare, and a narrow oak armoire and a brick-red-painted blanket chest took up most of the last one – along with a wooden folding screen to partition off some modest dressing space in the corner.

Scanning the room for signs of comfort, since it certainly held no luxury, she spotted two scrolled wrought iron grates, set into the wide floorboards directly over the coal stove and fireplace in the keeping room below. She surmised that living here could be relatively comfortable during the winter, if there were enough fuel. After all, most of her ancestors had lived frugally at one time or another. If this ancient woman could manage, so could she! She was jolted, then instantly amused, by the realization that she was seriously considering a long stay, whether or not her hostess proved senile. Childish and unrealistic it might be, but she was enchanted by the very thought of living here.

The Crone gently patted the right-hand bed. "Yours," she said.

So Augusta completed her inspection of the room -- her quarters, as she was coming to label it -- and was satisfied. Minimalist it certainly was, yet comfortable, cozy, friendly, easy, familiar ... she rolled the adjectives slowly across her mind. And the odor was just as Augusta expected: gently lavender.

Her hostess had disappeared outside by way of the Dutch door; Grumpkin, groaning grouchily (ecstatically), trotted and wagged beside her mistress.

Augusta stared wistfully at her new bed, then eagerly pulled back the quilt, exposing rough-spun sheets and a light wool blanket that were far too inviting. She kicked off her shoes and lay down gingerly, a little unsure of the rope supports. As she sank gratefully into the deep featherbed, her mind and body flooded with nostalgia, memories of the time in her life when she had known unconditional love – childhood visits with her grand-mother. Just what had triggered the feelings? So many things: the Crone's implicit acceptance of her, the quiet of the old house, the ancient furnishings, the smell of Sweet Fern and lavender. Yes, that was it. Expecting to savor this moment, as the down mattress lifted itself lightly around her, she was instantly asleep.

CHAPTER THREE

Augusta awoke without conscious effort, neither startled nor concerned to find herself in this unfamiliar bed, already half believing that she'd been involved in the activities of the stone house for years. Glancing around for a mirror and finding none, (she found it later, behind the screen) she patted her hair once or twice and hiked rapidly to the outhouse. It was a sturdy one-holer with an oval wooden cover that rested, hingeless, in place. The building's odor was quite passable, considering the warmth of the weather. She admired the thoughtful touch of a bowl of dried rose-petals and herbs in one corner, and was relieved to find several rolls of ordinary toilet paper next to the tin scoop and bucket of sand for scatter-covering the refuse.

She paused to admire the diminutive charm of the cottage from this angle – a slated, one-story hut with a single recessed window, a paneled but unpainted Dutch door, and just the slightest wisp of smoke rising from the coal-stove's chimney. Striding down the steep path to the left of the cottage, she found herself once again at the front door, noticing for the first time a couple of dishtowels slung over a short rope, tied between the doorjamb and the window's shutter.

CRONE; A Meditation on Womanhood

The Crone was seated on the longer of the two benches, her back quite straight, her hands laid lightly on her thighs with palms up, as if she were waiting to receive something. Her face at rest was even more deeply wrinkled and weathered than Augusta had first thought. The younger woman settled on a large, bench-like boulder, to enjoy the serenity of the surroundings, calming the bouncy Grumpkin with long, gentling strokes. The renewed screams of peacocks and alarms of geese failed to rouse her hostess. The aged woman's lips were parted slightly, and Augusta thought she heard, more than once, a whispered "Thank you," although her mouth surely had not moved; perhaps it was simply the sound of her exhaling breath.

A few minutes passed; the Crone opened her eyes languidly, as if she were still in some gentle dream, and peered at Augusta with a slight squint, smiling in recognition.

"You had a pleasant nap, too," Augusta said conversationally, alluding to her own comfortable rest.

The Crone denied it with a shake of her head. "Listening to life," she explained.

Augusta, who had recently begun to meditate in a somewhat haphazard, inconsistent fashion, was straightaway alert, thinking she must have misunderstood. "Pardon me, but did you say it was 'life' or 'love' that you were listening to?"

The woman-with-no-name cocked her head, narrowed her eyes. "Ah," she said at last. "Same thing."

The listener was totally unprepared for what happened to her next. She quite literally staggered under the power of that simple statement. Previously, such emotional impacts had always heralded a radical shift in her view of the world. It was happening again. No doubt! Life and love the *very* same? Why had she never known that before? But she had indeed known it, somewhere in the deepest room in her heart. How do such truths become buried? Much later, attempting futilely to explain the effect, conjuring up a few lame words that scarcely touched upon the depth of the experience, she had stretched out her arms in a mute gesture of joy.

CRONE; A Meditation on Womanhood

If the Crone noticed Augusta's turmoil, she failed to acknowledge it, engaged as she was in her own enjoyment of the cool shadow against the side of the house. The sun was past half-day, and already well hidden behind the roof of the cottage; the shade was a welcome relief. The original owners positioned the house to capture the morning sun full-face, forfeiting the pleasure of the mountain's sunsets – a matter of little importance, perhaps, but Augusta was disappointed when she realized it. Her mind played for several moments with the benefits of designing mountaintop houses with full-compass views, determining the relationship of the sun to bedroom windows, and so on.

"Peas and lettuce," were the Crone's very next words, interrupting Augusta's architectural daydreaming. The ancient woman's terse comment needed no further amplification. To her younger companion, it was clarity itself. Augusta lifted down a shallow wooden basket from a beam in the keeping room, and headed off toward the garden, more than ever perplexed by this day's experience – never having done this act before in this place, but knowing exactly what was expected of her and how to go about it. A strange reality I'm in, she was thinking, as she opened a chicken-wire gate and stepped into the tiny enclosure. Even the top of the garden was covered with wire netting to protect it from the peafowl. Augusta broke several handfuls of fresh new peapods from their vines, and placed them in her trug, piling a goodly stack of soft, red-leaf lettuce on top. It seemed early for beans, Augusta thought, but they were ready to pick. Perhaps the little valley allowed an early harvest.

Kneeling awkwardly – for Augusta was no gardener and her body was reluctant– she dug her fingers into the crumbling sun-warm soil, to tug weeds from the base of the lettuce and tomatoes, savoring for a long moment this contact with Mother Earth. Her thoughts leapt again to her elderly hostess, questions tumbling through her mind: the Crone's age, her ancestry, her means of support, who helped her care for this splendid little homestead? Surely she was unable to mow and rake and carry for herself.

CRONE; A Meditation on Womanhood

And who was the woodcutter? A fine high pile of split wood was methodically stacked against the stone sidewall of the cottage, covered over by a gray-green tarpaulin. The Crone was just now pulling down a single piece, cradling it in both arms, as she carried it back to the fireplace. The sight transported Augusta to her grandparents' home, where she knew the woodpile had been a certain sign of prosperity, security, and health. The year her grandfather died, Augusta, a ten-year-old child, had happened to walk alone behind their house, stunned to discover the pile of firewood unkempt, untended, unswept – a mere scattering of split logs and shredded bark. The life had gone out of it. She had wept for what seemed an extraordinary length of time, wondering, even at that young age, how a woodpile could touch her so deeply, when the crying of her mother and grandmother could not.

The sixty-three-year-old woman she had become sighed heavily. A part of her delighted in this endless store of memories, but another, more tender element, wished she had no history to dredge up, and so could avoid the loneliness, the heartache of remembered family past. A thin cloud shrouded the sun, darkening her world in seeming empathy, bringing with it a cooler, almost chill breeze, and the feel of a nearing storm. In the hills, the weather can veer off or reverse in an instant, ordinary warnings effectively hidden behind the trees and the next ridge.

She watched as the Crone disappeared into the house with another piece of firewood, returning momentarily to pull the towels down from their drying line. Augusta hurried, staggered, up the grassy hill to the Dutch door, one hand pressing the lettuce to keep it from blowing away, her hair challenged by the wind, her face splashed by several giant raindrops. She shut the two halves of the door firmly and latched them together, heart beating hard with exertion, but even more because of her childhood anticipation of the power of the storm. Then she remembered to pull the quilt up neatly on her bed. It would never do to be a careless guest, her long-dead mother was present to admonish.

By the time Augusta arrived in the keeping room, rain was dashing against the windows, and wind was shaking the ancient panes. The heat of the room declared that the coal stove had been stirred and fed; wood and kindling were laid, unlit, in the fireplace. The Crone welcomed her guest with a smile, but continued with her preparations, while Augusta placed a large mixing bowl in the sink, and added the peapods and lettuce for washing. She raised and lowered the water-pump handle several times, but felt little resistance. Without a second thought, she reached for the pitcher on the counter, filled it with water from the bucket on the floor and poured it steadily, rapidly, into the small rectangular hole. Five or six pumps later, water trickled and then gushed forth in a cold torrent. Augusta refilled the bucket before cleaning the vegetables, because she well-remembered that nothing is quite so irritating as to find that someone has allowed the priming water to run out.

In no time at all, a bowl of potato soup and a dinner plate were set at each place, along with cups for tea and sufficient mix-matched silver. The teapot steamed between them. A platter of lightly fried peapods, a salad bowl of greens and lemon juice, and a bowl of cut strawberries, their red outer skins contrasting deliciously with white flesh, completed the meal. The women seated themselves with a shared sense of sociable satisfaction, simultaneously bowing their heads. Augusta's prayer was short, but unrushed, beginning reverently with her secret, intimate name for the Creator, "Esse." She touched lightly on her experiences of the day and ended simply, "I am grateful."

Her eyes were still peacefully closed, and she was sure she hadn't spoken aloud, when, across the table from her, the Crone completed her own homage, and breathed in a strong whisper, "Thank you, Esse."

Augusta's eyes shot open in astonishment. "*What* did you say?" she managed to ask in a relatively calm voice.

"My Creator's name is Esse," she responded quietly, picking up her soupspoon, dipping it into the fragrant porridge and beginning to eat.

"So is mine!" Augusta replied in continued amazement. "May I ask you why?"

CRONE; A Meditation on Womanhood

The Crone looked at her openly, without guile. "Our reasons, the same," she replied.

But the other woman was caught up in an emotional whirlwind. Exhilarated, unwilling to release the subject, she began to tick off her own reasons:

"Esse is Latin for 'to be.' It instantly reminds me that we're all one being, one creative thought," she explained. "And Esse is always right *here.*" She touched her heart lightly with her fingertips. "When I say 'God,' I always imagine something harsh, judging and distant, but Esse is gentle and close. In fact, Esse is inside, and everywhere." The ancient one nodded, and Augusta inhaled calmly now, knowing that an explanation was truly unnecessary. The Crone understood.

"I really like the word, because it's always the same, backward, forward, even upside down -- just as Esse is constant and eternal." Again the Crone nodded, giving Augusta the impetus she needed to continue.

"And when I say 'Esse,' I know it isn't merely father or mother: Esse is so much more!" She paused to consider what point she might have missed. "Oh, yes. When I meditate, 'Esse' is like the sound of breathing – "*Ess,* inspiring – *Suh,* expiring. It's a lovely way for me to remember that Esse is Spirit."

Once again the Crone silently assented. At least, Augusta thought, her silence *seems* to be agreement, so she continued. "Most of all, when I began to use this new name, I was starting fresh – throwing out the judgmental us-against-them stuff I was taught." As she spoke, an ancient outrage rose inside her. "Even as a little child, I knew something was terribly wrong. First the church would say 'God is Love,' and then in the next breath, it was off into sin and judgment, attacking all those unsaved people who practiced other religions." Augusta paused again to calm herself, observing the Crone with a growing sense of connection.

"And don't forget the way women are put down! It makes me sick to think about all the cruel intolerance churches foist on the world. They talk about togetherness, but actually teach people how to hate anyone who's even a little different. But I'm absolutely sure that Esse has no favorites. None."

Augusta became thoroughly aware of her resentment and began to laugh at herself, finally dousing the heat of that emotional fire. "And here I am, being just as holier-than-thou! But, just one more thing..." (Augusta felt a desperate need to complete this idea), "... Esse is unconditional love, never needing to forgive or condemn. I suspect that Esse hasn't even the *concept* of forgiveness! I'm saying that my Esse is just about the complete reverse of everything I was taught." And she exhaled a burst of sharp laughter at her own vehemence.

"Oh, my! Excuse the lecture! I've just never shared Esse with anyone before, you know." And she looked into the Crone's eyes and saw that, indeed, she *did* know.

The old woman spoke for the first time. "And you?" she asked, with honest interest.

Augusta took the question to mean, 'Where are you in the scheme of things with this new understanding?' She sighed deeply, becoming silent for a long while as she ate her now-lukewarm potato soup. The crone waited with the patience of the old and wise.

"I know a couple of things now," Augusta answered at last. First, I'm powerless over everything in my life – and sometimes I can't stand it! What's really odd is this: at the very same time, I'm totally responsible for everything. And responsible to Esse." As she spoke, an expression of mischievous humor played across her face. "And sometimes I can't stand that either!" Laughter rose in her throat and spread into the room, joined by the deeper chuckle of the Crone. They looked at each other with satisfaction, with recognition, and finished their supper in silence, to the clatter of heavy rain on the slate roof.

*   *   *

CRONE; A Meditation on Womanhood

A voluminous, yellowing, granny nightgown lay neatly on Augusta's bed; the two women courteously took turns undressing behind the screen, the single kerosene lamp throwing huge shadows across the floor and walls. They were in bed soon after dark. It went unmentioned, but they expected to rise at daybreak.

"When do you usually go to sleep?" Augusta asked.

"After the whippoorwill calls," came the answer, but the storm continued well into the evening, and they expected nothing tonight. Augusta imagined the bird sitting glumly on a branch, or hiding in the dry, protected hole of a hollow limb. So close to the forest, far from the distractions of civilization, she was mindful of the earth's creatures, as she had never been before.

The Crone removed a flashlight from the bedside table's drawer, and placed it beside the kerosene lamp, where it seemed alien and garish among the old furnishings. She turned down the lamp, watching the wick descend slowly, until the white flame shrank and went out. The two women lay comfortable and secure in their rope beds, listening to the rumble-rattle of the rain, saying their customary prayers of blessings and thanks. Neither one could see a movement in the deep black, but the new houseguest had the slightest smile of childlike pleasure on her face. She could feel it. I wonder how many have slept in my bed, and felt as I do now?

Augusta was suddenly moved to make one last comment about Esse. "Mahm?" she called out in a half-whisper, unwittingly calling the old woman by a name that was somehow a blend of Mom and Ma'am, as the British might address the Queen. "Yes?" came the quiet answer.

"I don't believe in any kind of devil at all. We seem to have free will to do Evil. It's all our own stuff – ego or spirit. Blaming it on some thing else is just an excuse, a way to avoid our own responsibility. Do you know what I mean? Augusta wasn't sure why saying this was so important, but it was. She could feel the release of something inside her as she finished,

She was aware of the old woman settling in the bed, ropes creaking as they strained on their pegs. "Bless you," she replied, and to the younger woman it was a true benediction. A cat hopped onto her quilt and lay down against the back of her legs with the typical graceless flop that only a cat can effect. Probably Vincent, if she judged the weight correctly. It was soothing, this cat so readily accepting her presence . . . and the little homestead slept.

ACCEPTANCE

CHAPTER FOUR

Barest light of day; as the sun's glow slowly increased, Augusta lay contentedly in her rope bed, enjoying absolute serenity, her thin wool blanket keeping away the night's chill and the lingering damp of the storm. The pulse of life, inherent in the sound of waking birds, permeated mind and body – Esse as close and palpable as the air she breathed. Just as the rooster crowed beneath her window, she repeated her daily affirmation silently and with more than customary fervor and appreciation: *it's a glorious day.* Instantly her whole body shifted onto a higher, more secure and certain plane – as it always did when she repeated these words as a morning anthem of praise.

CRONE; A Meditation on Womanhood

"It's a glorious day." The echo -- aloud and older-voiced, but no less eloquent -- came from the far window next to the ancient woman's bed. The Crone was gazing at the brightening sunrise.

"Oh, you startled me! Good morning, Mahm. I had just said that very thing myself, and it sounds as if you read my mind," Augusta commented, in a voice that was about equal parts pure pleasure and annoyance.

"Unsurprising," the Crone replied with a good deal of certainty and satisfaction.

"How does she do that? She gets more wisdom and profundity into one or two words than I can manage in twenty!" Augusta said to herself as she slid from her bed and headed rapidly for the outhouse, which seemed a day's trek away. Still-chilly air and a clear sky promised a glorious morning indeed.

By the time she arrived in the kitchen, the coal stove had been brought to life, fed from the scuttle under the stairs, the Crone was contentedly soft-boiling eggs, and thick slices of dark, sprouted wheat bread and jam waited on the table. "Cider in the spring house," the old woman commented cheerfully, handing her guest a couple of heavy white mugs.

Augusta half-walked, half-slid down the rain-muddied path to the smaller stone building, pausing for a moment to admire the sun's ascent over the ridge. A single window let sunlight into the spring house. It's single room was damp, and empty except for a slow-moving clean-sandy canal that bordered two walls. Pure water seeped up from the depths of the mountain, was caught for a moment in this man-made trough, and released again through an underground pipe to the pond. Several crocks of varying sizes had been set in the cold water, and many overlapping rings in the sandy bottom marked its long-time use. It was a free, functional cooling system that guaranteed a constant temperature during the most bitterly cold or steamiest weather.

Augusta lifted the heavy pottery lid from a crock with a protruding ladle handle. Inside, the amber liquid was clear and inviting. A hesitant sniff and sip from the dipper proved she'd guessed correctly. While filling the mugs, she noticed that Vincent, curiosity aroused, had followed her in. "Come on, cat, I'm leaving!" She made kissing sounds to encourage the animal, wheedled "Vincent," and waited impatiently for a few moments before stepping outside, slowly pulling the plank door toward herself. As the springhouse became increasingly dark, the independent animal ambled across the doorsill, disinterested, as if it were his own unmotivated decision to depart.

Breakfast was silent and companionable, begun with heads bowed in common thanks, and punctuated by the territorial screams of the resident peacocks. Afterwards, the Crone brought forth a brand-new comb and toothbrush -- as if she frequently had unprepared guests -- along with soap and a somewhat frayed but clean towel. (How does she do laundry? Augusta wondered, not wanting to ask.) Partially filling a large, china bowl with hot water from the stove, she cooled it from the priming bucket. It was a difficult act for the old woman, but Augusta hardly noticed. I'm quite prepared to enjoy this frugal life, she was thinking – if only I can wash my hair by tomorrow!

Kitchen cleanup was quickly done with a minimum of wasted motion, the two women working independently but in tandem, at opposite ends of the keeping room. Completing their household tasks, drying their hands on stained waist-tied bib-aprons, they walked silently outside to the long bench, and sat down side by side, to listen for awhile to the rhythm of life. The risen sun shone full in their faces, and Augusta instantly felt herself a part of the homestead's undeviating daily devotional.

For a long moment, the younger woman observed the distant geese methodically washing themselves, scooping their heads under water with great undulating strokes, extending and shaking wet wings, greeting the day with squawking complaint. Slowly she closed her eyes, allowing her body to relax, becoming aware of her own rhythmic breathing. The noise of the mountain creatures continued around her, but she no longer gave them conscious attention. Instead, Augusta focused on the steady cadence of her breathing. Whenever her mind drifted, she pulled herself back to her breath, idly observing her thoughts as they drifted by. With every in-breath she thought "Esse," and her mind quieted. With every out-breath she repeated "Thank you." As the brain-chatter subsided, her mind became more tranquil, and her inner spirit was filled.

A half-hour passed in an instant for the Crone and her guest. They stirred at the same time, slowly opening their eyes, at once calmed and energized by their morning meditation. They returned to the bustle of the mountain retreat with vastly sharpened awareness, just as Grumpkin belatedly discovered she'd lost the center of attention. Quite the opposite of Vincent, the self-contained and independent cat, the puppy bounded toward the bench, agitating the hens into a whirl of frightened feathers, tail spinning, stout little body twirling out of control in her effort to be noticed.

Observing the puppy's frantic efforts, Augusta had a sudden, agonizing vision of herself as a little girl, all eyes and smiles and pert party dress, pirouetting for family or guests, especially the men, displaying herself like a china doll on a musical turntable. The torment on her face was so graphic that the Crone paused and cocked her head quizzically, with an expression of openly grave concern.

"Oh!" Augusta answered the unspoken question, "I just had an appalling vision ..." and she described the experience in some detail, plagued with conflicting emotions, remembering the adult smiles and applause, yet feeling underneath that she, the real Augusta, had actually been patronized, discounted, belittled, objectified and ...

"Invalidated," the Crone completed her thought with a bitter laugh.

"Yes, and they're still doing that to little girls, expecting them to prance and primp like wind-up dolls, instead of behaving like human beings. I had forgotten the horror of it, I suppose, because the applause seemed like flattering attention. It makes me sick to remember it! And even then, I had an inkling that it was cruel."

CRONE; A Meditation on Womanhood

The Crone began to mutter to herself, "Have you been a good girl, have you been a *good* girl ..." in a sing-song voice, while Augusta's mind combined "*nice* little girl" and "*nice* little puppy" into one mock-soothing comment. Suddenly the two women were chanting derisively:

> There was a little girl who had a little curl,
> Right in the middle of her forehead.
> When she was good, she was very, very good,
> And when she was bad, she was horrid.

They leaned back against the stone wall, filled with an uncontrollable laughter born of buried hurt and well-learned self-contempt (after all, what were little girls really *good* for?) and born, too, of the certain knowledge that such refined disdain persisted. Indeed, it was adult women, often led by the media, who foisted this perception upon their own kind, generation after generation, molding their willing, trusting girls into manageable round pegs. No wonder that a woman's self-esteem was all too often tenuous.

"But it *can* be different!" Augusta, out of breath, stopped long enough to assure her companion. "It's already different." She told the Crone of her own daughter, who had a sense of self far beyond her roles, who seemed to recognize her human individuality despite some of her mother's early, misguided attempts to mold and manage her.

The Crone gazed thoughtfully across the pond, then closed her eyes to summon her inner vision. "Perhaps," she acknowledged, with a nod symbolic of hope if not certainty, as the two women commenced a leisurely stroll around the pond, failing to notice any inconsistency, as they delighted in the Creator-defined roles of the animals in this miniature kingdom – peacocks a-scream, geese awash, puppy a slave to its co-dependent nature.

CHAPTER FIVE

The pond was swarming with activity. Turtles, five in a row on a warm rock, front feet perched on each other's shells, were playing fallen dominoes as they basked in the sun. Huge carp, their dark shadows barely moving in the shallow water, hung just beneath the surface, while frogs rested at the edge, bulging eyes blinking slowly and seldom. As the women passed by, the aquatic creatures dove, flipped or somersaulted out of sight, leaving a swirled trail of muddy streaks through the water.

The two walked slowly toward the fenced pasture, Vincent trotting beside them like a companionable dog, the Crone electing more than once to rest on a convenient rock or fallen log. A chestnut mare and her year-old filly trotted to the fence, eagerly awaiting some human attention, their heads far over the railing, lips puckered, stretching for a treat. The older woman felt around in the folds of her dress, and brought forth two sugar cubes, offering them on flattened, outstretched palms to the expectant animals, who lifted them away daintily, with moist, mobile lips.

Augusta inspected the horses. They were clean and curried, the mare's mane intricately braided and woven with a red ribbon – certainly not the work of the ancient crone. "What beautiful animals! Who takes care of them?" she asked, as she rubbed a gentle hand over the mare's warm, velvet nose.

"Coming now," the older woman replied, inclining her head toward the open meadow. Two figures were climbing toward them along the meadow's dirt trail, one a woman, young by Augusta's measure, dressed in a blue plaid shirt, jeans and sneakers, her short, tight-curled black hair bound with a wide ribbon. The young girl striding just behind her was in similar attire, but her hair, corn-rowed and tipped with golden beads, bounced against her cheeks and forehead.

Slung from their belt loops by colorful bandanas were handmade ceramic mugs – a practical touch, Augusta thought,

CRONE: A Meditation on Womanhood

when traveling along mountain streams in warm weather. The two, swinging along with a similar step and style that identified them as mother and daughter, waved and hurried toward the fenced pasture.

The mother hailed the Crone with a gentle hug of obvious affection, then quickly turned to introduce herself to Augusta. "Hi, I'm Linda. This is my daughter, Jennifer," she said, laying an arm around the girl's shoulders, and reaching out to shake Augusta's hand.

Greeting the two, Augusta took an instant liking to the mother's unaffected enthusiasm and energy. Jenny said a quick hello. "Call me Jenny," and climbed between the fence rails, obviously anxious to be with her filly. Both horses edged close to the young girl, nudging her playfully, nibbling insistently at her pants pockets. "Stop that, Molly!" Jenny spoke sternly to the mare, while pulling out large hunks of crisp raw carrot, watching both animals affectionately as they made loud, open-mouthed crunches of pleasure. Then she trotted off to the tiny barn, horses close behind -- "Not now, Liberty!" – closing the lower half of the stable door so that she could shovel and clean and spread new straw undisturbed.

The three women chatted contentedly on their walk back to the cottage for a cup of tea, the orange cat keeping pace and earnestly yowling his opinion on every subject. Augusta was savoring the delicious feeling of acquaintance renewed, rather than the usual awkwardness of new introductions. It was truly strange, since she had never met the young mother before.

Linda and the Crone settled themselves on the sunny bench, while Augusta went to search for refreshments. To her surprise, she discovered a warm teapot on the corner of the coal stove, tea steeped and strong, a kettle of hot water beside it, for diluting a too-potent brew, and a small plate of buttered bread strips and grapes, towel-covered to keep off tiny creatures with or without wings. The Crone had surely expected her guest.

Three generations of women sat sociably on the two benches, leaning against high wooden backrests that protected them from the rough cottage wall. They spoke, or were quiet in turn. No one felt the need to fill a silence until genuinely moved.

At one point, Augusta commented that the great majority of the Crone's many animals were female – except for her two favored orange cats, and Sneer. The eldest woman shrugged her shoulders. "Neutered," she said, sending the three into an explosion of laughter that ended in a Crone-coughing-fit.

A little later, Linda said, "I'd like to meditate with you." The others immediately closed their eyes, aware that this act was not so much ritual, as unspoken need -- for female connectedness, commonality, and spiritual support.

When they opened their eyes and drew their senses back to the homestead, it was just in time to see Jenny in the distance, sliding from a fence rail onto the bare back of the mare. She leaned down to lift the rope-latch, kicked the gate away with her foot, allowing the horse to sidle out of the paddock, followed closely by the filly, whose only attachment was her mother's love.

Augusta inhaled sharply, disconcerted. No bridle? No saddle? No trappings of control? Linda explained that her daughter rode Indian fashion, and was even now learning their training techniques, to communicate with her horse, rather than dominating her. "Jenny's ten. I want her to take pride in her discipline and skill, so when she gets to high school, and they try to make her merely another girl, and a black one at that, she'll already have enough inner strength to maintain her self-esteem."

"Are schools really like that ... still?" Augusta was dismayed.

"Yes, they are." Linda responded. "I teach fifth grade. The girls are bright and verbal, filled with wonder. Bigger than the boys, learning quicker, knowing they can do anything -- absolutely no limits. But in high school something happens. Many studies show how teachers – men and women alike – methodically undermine the confidence of teen-age girls, while actively *urging* to boys to excel. It doesn't have to be conscious or malicious, you know, but it's terribly hard to counteract; the message weighs a girl down until her self- esteem can crumble."

CRONE; A Meditation on Womanhood

Augusta nodded, remembering. "My parents always assured me I could *be* anything I wanted to be, and *do* anything I set my heart on. Later on, I discovered that the world expected me to want only what girls were *supposed* to want – and girls weren't really supposed to have ambition."

"My mother," Augusta went on, "also tried to make me behave properly, to *socialize* me. She sure had a job! Defiance was my middle name." Startled at her comment, she paused. "Hmm -- probably still is!" She laughed at herself. "Anyway, my mother would tell me, "It isn't done!" whenever I tried to break out of the 'good girl' mold – or even put my feet on the sofa. I never understood how she knew what *was* done and what wasn't. Anyway, they felt like conflicting messages -- kept me off-balance when I was growing up."

The three stared at the pond for a long while, waiting for Augusta to complete her thought: "By the time I was ten or so, I had wings! Then, a few feathers got clipped when I wasn't looking, in the name of 'being practical,' I suppose. I never learned where balance is, between doing the everyday drudge things and reaching for the dream.

The others laughed. They hardly need mention it was "woman's work" that could sidetrack a life, if you let it.

Augusta sat back with a smile. Thank heaven for mothers like you, Linda!"

The young woman nodded. "I have a boy, too. I want them both to be free to follow their dream, and develop their own talents, regardless."

With that, she tore a grape in two, tossing the pieces to a peacock that had strolled hopefully close. He ate the sweet fruit in a single, pecking gulp, then shook his tail in what must have seemed, to him, a flattering response. It lifted and fanned into a glorious display of iridescent green and blue eyes. Linda tore and tossed another grape, but the peacock was too full of himself to go after it. A gray peahen, hesitant at first, scooted in and snatched the food away, leaving the hungry male to pirouette alone, his sail-tail throwing him off-balance in the sudden breeze. "So like a man," the Crone remarked.

" ... And so like a woman!" Linda completed the thought, sending the trio off into another round of laughter.

Hugging both women, she waved a cheerful good-bye as she headed toward the pasture. "See you at the Gathering."

Jenny cantered up to the fence on the mare, with Liberty close behind. A while later, mother and daughter hiked off, turning to wave just before disappearing behind the meadow rim. The Crone returned the salute with arms up-stretched -- hail, blessing and farewell wrapped in that single gesture.

"Imagine training your own horse!" Augusta had been visualizing herself in Jenny's place, noticing her own exhilaration. The words of the Crone, who had stepped into the cottage ahead of her, drifted back. "Strong woman."

"She certainly will be," Augusta agreed. "I wonder. Does Jenny realize yet how lucky she is to have a mother like that?" Or was the Crone describing Linda?

CHAPTER SIX

The Crone set out a light lunch of the remaining bread, strawberries and grapes, and asked Augusta to fetch cider from the springhouse, as well as some celery and a half-cabbage (to add crunch to the meal).

After they had seated themselves and given thanks, Augusta asked about Linda's casual remark. "What is this about a Gathering?" already thinking of it with a capital "G," knowing that it was to be an important event, certain that she would get only the barest of answers from her minimal-mouthed hostess.

"Summer solstice," came the Crone's reply, in a tone that implied her guest ought to have known the significance of the date.

"And who will be here?" Augusta pressed on.

"Village women and great-granddaughters," came the crisp reply, but with the barest of satisfied smiles behind it.

Sensing that the Crone was treating it as a splendid surprise, and that all would unfold in its proper time, her houseguest sighed, surrendered, and dropped the questioning, even about great-granddaughters. She would just have to wait, whether patiently or not.

As she rinsed and dried the mugs and lunch plates, and wiped the oak table with a damp cloth, all the while she was observing the old woman out of the corner of her eye, as she gathered together vegetables, utensils and bowls. "What are we having for supper, Mahm?" Augusta finally asked.

The Crone merely shrugged her shoulders and made an expansive gesture toward the low shelf of staples on the back wall. Augusta had not studied the contents of the various crocks and jars so neatly lined up, but she could see the yellow glint of dried corn through the green glass of one, and the light sheen of brown rice through the clear side of another. Everything to survive a long, isolated winter, she couldn't help thinking.

To watch the Crone at work was a lesson in itself. Old and slow and used to doing chores alone, she had obviously made peace with her physical limitations. Rather than filling the kettle at the pump, lugging it, then heaving it, heavy and awkward onto the coal stove, she brought several pitchers-full to the pot. Augusta recalled having seen the Crone manage firewood in much the same manner – one piece at a time. Instead of shifting bulky jars and crocks, the low shelf gave the ancient woman the ability to tip them where they sat, scooping out the contents and returning them to their upright positions. Necessary, practical, and good exercise!

The Crone took three hanging onions down from the beam, and handed Augusta celery, cabbage and a brittle, twisted brown stick that transformed into a pliable sheet of brown-green seaweed after a brief soaking. The younger woman cut it into small strips and placed them in a bowl, along with the sliced celery, onions and cabbage she had methodically prepared.

Into the pot, already simmering on the stove, the elder woman dumped a large scoop of barley, a cup of lentils – Augusta's children called them "fuzzy peas" – and a scoop of black beans that had been soaking in cold water since the night before. She tipped a palmful of curry into the steaming pot, and directed Augusta to add the sliced vegetables. "Nap now, carrots later," she remarked, looking tired but satisfied, as the two ascended to the second floor. The Crone, climbing more slowly than before, had difficulty avoiding a bouncy Grumpkin, who had just learned how to navigate the stairs, and needed to demonstrate the new skill several times.

CHAPTER SEVEN

The two women woke from their longish naps to the pungent odor of onions, cabbage and curry – and the gleeful barking of the puppy, who was bumping down the stairway, apparently managing several treads at once. "Hey, there, Grumble," came the voice of a young woman, followed by a light thump, as the new arrival gently dropped two canvas carryalls on the table. No paper or plastic bags for this earth-conscious household. She had carried in the Crone's groceries, and, her weekly laundry, carefully folded.

"Andrea," the Crone explained the visitor. By the time the two women had "refreshed themselves" (as Augusta's grandmother had always said), and descended to the keeping room, a bowlful of carrots had been cleaned and cut into curious triangular shapes, ready to add to the simmering pot. The few perishables had been hidden away in their springhouse crocks.

Augusta heard the rhythmic *whump* of a sledgehammer splitting wood, and knew it must be Andrea at work. Although it hadn't been said, women supporting women was the clear purpose of the stone cottage, and surely only another woman would be working here. Augusta laughed to herself, to think that she had once wondered if the old woman was lonely!

She tipped the odd carrot pieces into the pot with hardly a splash. Lifted lid sent the aroma of curry and cabbage through the keeping room, causing the women to glance at each other, grinning with happy anticipation. Just at that moment, Andrea thrust her head in at the door and said "Hey!" in a hearty voice. The Crone reached out scrawny arms and tilted a wrinkled cheek for a hug and a peck. The visitor was smaller than Augusta had imagined, considering the labor she performed here. About thirty, Andrea had a ballet dancer's lithe and wiry body, straight black hair to her waist, and a classically beautiful, high-browed Oriental face.

They introduced themselves informally, Augusta instantly feeling the same sense of previous acquaintance that she'd experienced on meeting Linda. She marveled at the strength of this common thread, that was the Crone's tangibly unconditional acceptance of people. In this wise old woman's presence, one felt no need to "put on airs," as Augusta's grandmother would have described it, or to gild the truth.

The ensuing conversation was an example. She had brought mugs of steaming herb tea outside to the two older women, whose bench was already shaded from the afternoon sun. Now she settled down on the still-sunlit-boulder before them, one leg bent, fingers linked around her knee, rocking slowly, her gaze concentrated on the ground in front of her.

"You're not yourself," the Crone observed.

"No, I'm not, Mahm. I have a serious problem," she began abruptly. Augusta registered only the slightest surprise that she was willing to speak of personal problems in front of a stranger, (and using the same form of address that the middle-aged matron had instinctively employed.) "I think I'm pregnant." Andrea rocked to and fro, looking steadfastly at the grass, then lifted her eyes slowly, tears of disbelief and anger in her eyes. "He's married, but he wants me to have the baby. I still can't believe I fell for it. He *told* me he had such a low sperm count that it was perfectly safe. What a rotten bastard!"

"What do *you* want?" the Crone asked quietly.

The question slowed down long enough for her to answer. "I know I don't want to have a child. I can't afford it. I don't trust him to support us, and I can't take care of a baby right now. I'm finally going to college – a baby would ruin everything." She sounded as if she'd been memorizing the points in support of her argument, but the underlying truths shone through nonetheless.

She searched both faces for sympathy, but saw only acceptance. "So he won't pay for an abortion, and I can't help feeling it's all his damned fault!" she continued, becoming more righteously indignant. "Don't you think he should *do* something?"

The two older women shook their heads. "Your responsibility," said the Crone gently. Augusta went on, "It would be nice if he did, but the ultimate choice is always yours. *Your* body; *Your* life; *You* gambled, and now you've got the consequences. If you *have* the child, he can help support it."

"But he *told* me ......" protested.

"Just who is responsible for the pregnancy?" Augusta interrupted.

"We both are," came the too-quick reply.

But Augusta shook her head once sharply. "That's a cruel hoax dumped on women -- trying to make us innocent victims. The truth is, only the woman can choose whether or not to be a mother -- unless it's truly against her will. If you don't want to get pregnant, you protect yourself."

Andrea only nodded. She sipped her tea thoughtfully, sadly, and gazed out across the pond. "Yes, I do know that," she said quietly. "I think I'm more furious with myself than anything." And here the conversation ended, the three women sitting still,

CRONE; A Meditation on Womanhood

emotionally separated, but yearning to be something more to each other, each acknowledging in her own heart the ultimate loneliness of responsibility.

Only a short while later, Andrea appeared relaxed and cheerful. While eating a solitary bowl of stew in the keeping room, she had obviously come to some conclusion, although she made no mention of it. Moving quickly through the homestead, she completed her chores – a stack of fresh wood, sand in the outhouse pail, a full coal scuttle, kerosene lanterns replenished – and collected the Crone's small pile of laundry, pocketing her paycheck and the meticulously written list of items to be delivered on Friday. "Everything will be done in time for the Gathering," Andrea assured the Crone, giving her a quick hug. "I've fixed a box and blanket for Miss Priss next to the stove. I'll bet she has her kittens before I get back. Oh, and thank you both for your honesty. I needed it." Off she went, following Linda's and Jenny's earlier route down the meadow trail.

The older women, watching her disappear over the ridge, whispered short prayers for her safety and protection. "No Prince Charming," the Crone sighed, "... and no Fairy Godmother, either," Augusta finished the thought. "When are women going to get the message that we're totally responsible for our own lives?"

"I'm glad we agree, my dear," the Crone replied, patting Augusta's hand in recognition of their common frustration.

"Oh, so much!" the younger woman was vehement.

They sat quietly together for a very long time, thinking of Andrea, and Miss Priss the pregnant cat, and the wonderful, fearful burden of their own motherhoods.

Soon their minds shifted to the uncomplicated joys of being a grandmother – simple joys of cuddling and cookies, peekaboo and reading aloud. Who could have foretold how the fears of motherhood would be marvelously transformed into the wisdom and simplicity of becoming grandmothers?

I'm a great-great-grandmother," the ancient woman said softly, some poignancy in the inflection of her voice causing Augusta to study the altered expression on her face. "Me!" the old

CRONE; A Meditation on Womanhood

one said, both hands laid upon her breast in a gesture of such gratitude that Augusta was stunned. And yet she perceived that the 'great-great-grands' were only part of the gratitude; the Crone's passion stemmed from her appreciation of all Esse's gifts – her love of family, her own lengthy survival in good health, and yes, the miracle of life itself.

They caught each other's eye for just a moment, and grinned, knowing they were thinking similar thoughts. Augusta broke the silence first. "People joke about how much better it would be if we had our grandchildren first! But it's really true for me. I'm only now, at sixty-three, learning how to love without judging, because of my grandchildren. I feel truly blessed. I don't order them around like I did my own kids. They're just energetic, happy children exploring their world. I can lead without demanding. How I wish I'd been as patient and understanding with my own children!"

Augusta continued to reminisce, realizing that she was almost afraid to acknowledge the full truth of her blessings. Did she think they might be taken away from her if she valued them too much? Her three children were a blessing, but, when they were young, she'd been so anxious to *bring* them up right that she'd missed most of the daily pleasures of their *growing up!* And how often had she self-centeredly brushed them off when they interrupted her, because she was "too busy?" She exhaled a long, deep sigh of regret as she remembered those long-ago days.

The Crone suddenly recalled a song-poem that her granddaughter had written about her several years ago. "Wait," she said, getting up with great difficulty, pushing with all her strength against one arm of the bench to recover her balance. She returned with a fragile piece of paper that she handed to Augusta with obvious pride:

THE PEACOCK COTTAGE

When I was a young girl, an innocent child,
I dreamed all those good days away,
With visions of gleaming white horses,
And a prince who would take me to stay
In a castle surrounded by peacocks,
Their tails fanned in gaudy display.

All too soon I became a young mother,
And I dreamed all those good days away
With visions of three perfect children
And a time when we'd all go to stay
In a castle surrounded by peacocks,
Their tails fanned in gaudy display.

Then my children grew up and they left me,
For dreams of their own far away,
With visions of three perfect households,
Yes, a time when they'd all go to stay
In their castles surrounded by peacocks,
Their tails fanned in gaudy display

Now I'm older and wiser by far,
I don't dream these good days away;
My children have children have children,
Now with grandma they sometimes will stay,
In my cottage – surrounded by peacocks –
Their tails fanned in gaudy display.

"This is wonderful," Augusta said, handing the worn paper back to the Crone. A peacock screaming in the distance punctuated her point. "Aren't we lucky we've learned at last to pay attention to the moment? It's a true grandmother's song. I have five grandchildren myself. How about you?"

CRONE; A Meditation on Womanhood

The elderly woman thought for a while before answering. "Three children, eleven grandchildren, thirty-seven great-grandchildren – and sixty-four, or maybe five, great-great grandchildren."

"Are they all living?" Augusta was curious.

"All but two," came the reply, "and all healthy."

Augusta started to say 'how marvelous,' reflexively, when the full impact of that population explosion hit her. My God, the Crone was responsible for 113 living people on this tiny planet! So many babies used to die as infants, at least in this country. No longer. They live .... and they multiply! "How marvelous," remained stuck, unsaid, in her throat.

"Far too many." The Crone continued, seeming to read her mind again.

"Yes." Augusta hesitated. "I'm sure they're wonderful people," she said apologetically, but ..." she was compelled to continue, "the earth is too delicate; too many mouths to feed; too much sewage; polluted drinking water; toxic waste; poisoned oceans. She's collapsing after all."

Indeed, the enormous number of the Crone's living relatives had profoundly shocked her, had brought home with a terrible immediacy the horror of overpopulation – humankind careening out of control. The earth was already in the throes of dying, and all too few people seemed to know it, or understand the need for action. "It's too late!" the words hammered her brain. "Too late! Too late!"

But she heard the Crone saying softly, "We will change our ways."

Augusta focused on the Crone's face. "*Who* will do it?" she queried sharply. "Mankind continues to laugh at all the warnings."

"Women," the ancient one replied, the truth of a prophet reverberating in her voice. "Mothers will save Mother Earth."

Something stirred deep in Augusta's soul as she heard "Mother" spoken with such love and reverence, evoking our exquisite planet as the nurturing presence she truly is, rearing and tending us, giving us all that we need for life. Augusta stared at the Crone in speechless astonishment, as a pinprick of white light, of hope rekindled, swelled and caught fire in her heart. She knew that the Crone's answer was the only one that made sense – if indeed there was to be any answer at all. It was the *only* chance. It *had* to be so. And, with a sudden flash of prescience, Augusta realized that the Gathering was to be the genesis.

CHAPTER EIGHT

While the Crone basked in her view of meadow and mountains from her bench, Sneer sprawled to overflowing on her lap, Augusta took a leisurely stroll around the pond, observing Mother Earth in some of her countless, delightful forms: a turtle rising silently from the murky depths to paddle toward shore, a dapple-brown bunny frozen in fright beneath his bush, a wedge of Canada geese overhead, honking flight signals as they migrated toward their evening's waterhole.

She stopped, surprised, when she came upon several barn swallows playing Feather-Catch in the air. What an enchanting sport! A single bird swooped to the ground, gathering in its bill a soft, curling white goose feather, then rose and wheeled gracefully over the pond, giving one last flippant turn before dropping it. As the feather seesawed gently toward earth, a second bird dove forward, catching it, lifted it a few feet, only to drop it again as a third swooped in. This shuttlecock was caught and served five times before landing at last in the water. One of the players searched for a new one, rejecting a feather that was too heavy or stiff, and the game resumed.

Augusta walked to the pulse and spirit of the mountains, consciously trying to avoid all thoughts of the destruction she

CRONE; A Meditation on Womanhood

knew was being perpetrated in the name of "progress," just on the far side of the ridge. She felt fearful and helpless, even though her talk with the Crone had ignited some new hope. *Could* women work together after all? What was woman's purpose? She remembered the old disparaging saw: "to cook, to clean, and to care." Menial, mundane jobs at best. Restoring the health of the earth would take an absolute commitment, the combined will of the whole human species, a total turnabout in life-styles and desires. What a preposterous fantasy! Augusta knew how inconvenient it was just to separate her own garbage for recycling. Yet she was now extraordinarily aware that her every act affected every *one* and every *thing*. It was no longer mere metaphor that we are all one, interconnected.

Staring into the pond-water, bursting with life, she wondered what concealed damage had already been done here in these peaceful hills, not far enough from the waste products of "advanced" civilization – toxins in the deep aquifers, pollution in the air, corrosion from acid rain. When Augusta noticed a haze of deepening pink on the surface of the muddy pond-mirror, she was half-willing to believe that Mother Earth had begun to hemorrhage in distress. Women to plant , to cleanse and to heal her? That was an inspirational way to view it, but motivating a generation of women? It seemed ludicrous indeed.

Released from her troubling fantasies, she discovered that the sky was awash with broad strokes of mauve and fuchsia. On the far side of the pond, above the cottage, layers of clouds were edged in burnished bronze and gold, the stone house itself a darker blotch of gray shadow beneath the hill, as the sun sank far to the left of the cloud mass. Why hadn't Esse placed those clouds directly over the sun for the most glorious effect, she wondered with mounting irritation, as she headed back along the sloping path to the cottage.

"I wish the mountain weren't in the way – the sunset's so magnificent," Augusta said as she came up to the Crone.

"Past the outhouse," the old woman replied, with her customary dearth of words, waving her hand toward the back of the cottage. Without slowing her pace, the younger woman shifted direction into the shadows. She strode rapidly past the outhouse, noticing for the first time that the path, well-raked and cleared, was wide enough to walk two abreast. Someone else traveled this path often, and it was unlikely to be the old woman.

The climb was gradual, but Augusta was overweight and under-exercised, and the effort began to tell on her. Pines stretched black and austere on either side, edged in a sharp, rosy glow, brighter where the trees thinned out at their uppermost boughs. The forest floor was a thick bed of pine needles, with very little underbrush to hide the splendor of the evening.

At long last, the trail widened into a clearing, at the edge of a precipice; the sky was transformed into a blaze of sumptuous colors so overwhelming to the senses that Augusta gasped, shielding her eyes to defend herself from too much magnificence. Fingers widespread, she stretched involuntarily toward the sky, rotating slowly, absorbing the glory into her body, laughing with a great shout of elation as the feeling of rapture swelled within her.

But euphoria receded as the sunset dimmed. The flaming ball slipped rapidly behind the next mountain, carrying with it the brightest colors, leaving the clouds in softer, grayer shades of mauve. Augusta was delighted to realize that Esse had moved the clouds directly over the sun for a more perfect sunset – as if a sunset could ever be less than perfect, she hastily reminded herself.

Against an outcropping of rock, someone had built a glorified sleeping bench for four, with a high back and roof that allowed a panoramic, yet protected, view of the broad valley and the undulating wave of deep purple mountains beyond. It was already evening in the village of Miraton; every few moments another light winked on in the deeply shadowed valley. Augusta climbed onto the platform and leaned against the back of the seat, glowing with the last pink of the sunset, and imagined what it would be like to sleep here – not alone, she quickly decided, hearing the rustle of a wild animal in the silence.

At the far edge of the clearing, a giant tree trunk loomed tall and stark against the sky, its top a mass of huge, jagged splinters – all that was left of a pine that had been snapped off in a severe storm. From the stumps of its remaining branches hung bunches of dried flowers, feathers tied with strips of rawhide, a leather drawstring pouch; a candle sat on a broken branch, wedged into a small hole; a withered garland of flowers and grasses swung slightly in the dying breeze above a birch-bark trencher of corn. The meaning of the shattered pine escaped Augusta. That it was a totem or an altar of sorts was clear, but why in this place? Despite the mystery, she stood for a moment before it respectfully. Something about the broken tree was imposing, even commanding.

Just before it was too dark to notice, her eyes rested on a small grave, marked with light-colored stones: JON. She knew without ever being told that it was the place of a beloved small child, remembered forever, but perhaps not spoken of, often, because the pain was too great.

The sky darkened rapidly. Augusta headed back down the path through the pines, curiously undisturbed by shadows moving among the indistinct tree trunks. At times she could just make out the light of a kerosene lantern through the open door of the bedroom, apparently flickering, as her view shifted through the intervening branches.

Suddenly a whippoorwill, catching the last light of day, called from the trees near the totem seat. "Whip-poor-*will*," the sharp, flute-whistle phrase was repeated, with its characteristic upswing on the final note. Rooster at dawn -- whippoorwill at dusk. How perfectly lovely, Augusta thought. Free alarm clocks as part of the service. I've lost a lot, moving so close to town.

Ahead of her on the path, several dark shadows moved, paused, and stirred again. Augusta stopped, instantly more alert than fearful, allowing her eyes to become accustomed to the dusk, looking off to the side of the shadows to discern their true shapes. A sharp snort! Augusta jumped in spite of herself. The startled deer turned tail, flipping flashes of white as they trotted off a little way into the pines, then paused to look back at her.

The Crone, accompanied by the ever-bouncing Grumpkin, was waiting at the bedroom door, ready to shut and latch it behind her. Augusta was eager to share her overflowing emotions. "So magnificent!" she began breathlessly, speaking of the sunset, explaining how Esse had obligingly moved the clouds to make a more perfect composition. The Crone cocked her head and looked her in the eye. "Who moved?" she asked pointedly, and Augusta, catching the profound significance of the question, answered sheepishly, "I did, of course."

CHAPTER NINE

The vegetable stew had been ready a long while on the back burner. This old-fashioned stove, Augusta reflected, was truly ideal for cooking. A small fire in one corner gave the option of high heat for boiling water, while the rest of the surface was a cook-artist's palette – an infinite variety of temperatures. Rather than altering the heat of a single burner, the chef merely moved the pan or kettle to another spot. And small amounts of trash could be disposed of with a flick of the handle, inserted in one of the hot iron discs above the fire.

The two women spoke their gratitude over their meal. The brown gravy was punctuated with lighter barley-flecks and bright orange carrot chunks, some shaped like curved pyramids – if that's possible, Augusta said to herself. Slices of sprouted-wheat bread and butter, and wedges of orange, were spread on a small willowware platter, between mugs of clear spring water; the vase of meadow flowers had been replenished by Andrea, Augusta supposed. She closed her eyes for another moment of thanks, never in her life having felt more alive and content than at this moment.

CRONE; A Meditation on Womanhood

"An extraordinary thing happened on the way back from the sunset, Mahm," Augusta said. "I met a herd of deer – or, I should say, the deer and I met – and they didn't run away. You know how dark it was, but they stopped and watched me; wary, but not really fearful. It was altogether eerie, all of us walking in the woods together."

"Vegetarian?" The Crone asked.

"Why, yes. I've been strictly vegetarian for several years now – usually not even milk products, butter or eggs."

"Why?" The old woman questioned her.

"Many reasons. I've switched over slowly, because it's such a radical change in attitude. About ten years ago, I stopped eating red meat, partly because of the price, but also because I just felt uncomfortable after I ate it. Besides, my cholesterol was high." The Crone nodded, listening intently as she ate her supper.

"After that, my husband had liver cancer, and the doctor recommended a macrobiotic diet. He said sticking to vegetables was healthier – more bulk, vitamins, minerals – and none of the empty sugar and fat calories Len loved so much. The doctor told us that researchers, in the late 1930's, had discovered that avoiding meat might minimize the pain of cancer, but doctors ignored that fact when chemo came along. It seems they just can't make money recommending a vegetarian diet."

Augusta went on: "I began to feel better, little aches and pains left, I woke up easily in the morning, lost some cravings . . . that kind of thing. But after Len died, I got back into the habit of eating poultry. Then I moved to the country. I have a pond on the other side of this mountain with ducks and geese, and a rooster named 'Popeye,' short for 'chicken popeye,' you understand?" The Crone shook her head at the disgraceful pun.

"Once I got to know the personalities and habits of the birds, I lost that taste too. No more eating Esse's beautiful creatures! And the last straw was learning that two thirds of our grain feeds animals so that we can eat their flesh later on. A horrible waste. So that's the story, Mahm. You probably heard much more than you expected to!" And Augusta dove into her stew, delighted with its texture and taste, pronouncing it delicious, not surprised to notice that, once again, she was doing all the talking and letting her food grow cold.

"How did we get started on this topic?" she continued curiously. "Ah, I remember. The deer." She looked quizzically at the Crone for an explanation.

"Not a carnivore," the ancient one replied, as she cleared the table.

Augusta had a flash of understanding. "You mean I don't smell like a meat eater!" I never heard that before, but it makes sense to me." She sat for a moment, recalling that, in their chance meeting, there had been no hunter and no hunted. It was gratifying to consider.

While the Crone finished the dishes, Augusta lit the small fire, pulling both wing chairs around to face it, the chill of the evening already penetrating the cottage. The old woman lowered herself slowly into the chair with a weary sigh, and laced her fingers together above her belly in a gesture that was a curious combination of self-satisfaction and reverence. Augusta joined her, and within moments their laps were enthusiastically cat-filled. Behind them, in the corner by the stove, came the scratch-and-twist sounds of Miss Priss preparing to settle into her birthing box.

The Crone, looking more ancient than ever as the firelight accentuated the wrinkles of her face, gazed into the fire or dozed, her head jerking upright from time to time, as she pulled herself back to the company of her guest. Several times she rubbed and squeezed her wrists and the swollen knuckles of both hands, her face distorted with pain. She sighed. "Another storm brewing."

Augusta, staring into the small blaze, was thinking how tranquilizing it all was – the warmth, the silence, the wave and flicker of the dim light. As she had often done as a child, she was imagining herself in miniature, walking through rosy-red caverns of burning logs, impervious to the flames, climbing steep, rough bark-slopes and leaping across chasms.

CRONE; A Meditation on Womanhood

She made a cup of bedtime tea for herself and her hostess. "Please," she said, "tell me the history of the shattered pine."

The Crone gathered herself together, sat up a little straighter. "The village," she began, "marked my location by the sentinel pine. When it disappeared, they thought I'd died." She paused to recollect the experience. "Well, it *was* a stormy night!" She smiled at the memory. "Trees down everywhere. In the morning they came ... worried ... drank up all the tea!"

The two sat in silence for several minutes, the Crone recalling the villagers' demonstration of friendship and love, Augusta visualizing the fear and anxiety of the women running toward the stone cottage.

"Thank offerings." the Crone finally continued, her voice growing weaker with the effort of so much talk. "Are they still there?" Augusta nodded, too moved by the simple story to speak.

"Haven't seen it," the Crone went on, "but I like the idea. Very much."

"And so do I," Augusta nodded, thinking to herself again: And so do I.

CHAPTER TEN

"It's a glorious day." Augusta silently repeated her ritual of greeting and gratitude, although the bedroom windows rocked and rattled with gusts of wind, and she could feel more than hear a far-off rumble of thunder somewhere in the mountains.

"Glorious day," the Crone remarked cheerily, on cue. "My bones felt it," she went on, alluding to the approaching storm, and kneading her hands one against the other. Suddenly a series of sharp, anxious whimpers from the keeping room alerted them both. "Where's Grumpkin?" she asked, moving as fast as her ancient limbs would take her.

The puppy, usually so active and irrepressible, paced and whined near the coal stove. The Crone rushed to the birthing box, crooning, "Priss, Priss," in an anxious tone. She sat down awkwardly, heavily, on he dirt floor beside the box, taking care not to frighten the little mother, who had never liked to be touched – although her dark eyes, enormous and dilated against white fur, seemed more trusting than usual.

Augusta stood on the far side of the box to watch, as the old woman reached in to scratch the cat comfortingly behind an ear. Priss leaned into the touch and began to purr, a strong, rhythmical sound of surprising strength. The Crone, who was leaning over the box in an awkward position, asked Augusta to help her up. She put her hands around the old woman's waist and half-lifted her into a kneeling position. What happened next so moved Augusta with its primal power that her chest tightened and tears blinded her eyes.

The Crone, with some sixth sense of motherly under-standing, and years of previous midwifery, became both physically and emotionally an extension of the animal. She placed her blue-veined hands on either side of the cat's head and stroked firmly, without pressing, down both sides of the furry body from her whiskers along the ribs and stomach to her thighs – repeating the motion again and again, each rhythmic stroke takng more than five seconds. Priss responded by turning over on her back and moving sensually, luxuriantly, while the sound from her throat swelled until it was no longer purr but ecstatic song . . . and a sac-enclosed kitten rose effortlessly and painlessly from her body to lie on her belly. "Ah!" the women exhaled in unison.

Priss curled over her tiger-striped child to begin the instinctive ritual of cleaning the slippery-wet baby, while Augusta awkwardly attempted to pull the ancient midwife to her feet. The two of them, off-balance, landed heavily on the floor, laughing and groaning as they tried to stand, the Crone incapable of managing

CRONE; A Meditation on Womanhood

alone. "I hate helpless," she muttered under her breath as she half-heartedly brushed herself off.

Breakfast was a leisurely affair of slow-cooked Irish oatmeal with raisins and dried apples, herb tea and pink grapefruit halves. The women said little, both enjoying this latest marvel in the constantly renewing miracle of birth. Grumpkin, puppy though she was, had become an anxious watchdog, sniffing over the edge of the box-cradle, her entire body vibrating in riveted enthusiasm.

Augusta peered into the carton and caught Miss Priss's eye. When she scratched an ear in congratulation, the new mother nudged her hand, clearly urging the woman to give her the same mid-wifely attention once again. Augusta was thrilled and fearful, but eager to help. She provided long, slow strokes. The cat responded, her purr again swelling into melodic song as another wet. membrane-packaged kitten came to rest on her stomach. Within a few moments, she was nursing a tricolor with large splashes of white, brown and orange.

The middle-aged woman sat down ponderously in one of the wing chairs, throat constricted with tears that could not be held back. The Crone waited patiently, knowing that Augusta would share her feelings once she caught her breath, but it was some little time before she was able to compose herself.

"Whew! I didn't expect that!" she exclaimed. "It brought up every emotion I've ever felt about giving birth! All I could think of was having my three children in a damned hospital with white-masked faces all around. No friends; only pain and a miserable hard bed and those obscene stirrups. I just felt so envious of Priss for having *us!*" And Augusta began to weep again, she supposed for women everywhere who had been robbed of their natural motherhood, of being cared for by other women in friendly, domestic surroundings. "I know it's getting better now, with midwives and all, but we have such a long way to go before we really get our sisterhood back!"

Augusta took a deep breath and sat up in surprise. "Why, I had no idea I felt like that," she said, clearly thrown off balance by the force of her feelings. "I would've thought I believed in sanitary hospital conditions and all that, but it's just not true. Women need to support each other in womanly things, but often we don't – too passive or sold a bill of goods – and we end up isolated from each other." She paused to catch her breath. "You're an amazing influence, Mahm," she said with return good humor. "You bring out the truth in me."

"Without trying," the Crone responded with a shrug and a smile.

CHAPTER ELEVEN

The storm had overtaken the cottage, wind whipping trees, rain beating windowpanes with unexpected ferocity. Augusta slipped an old yellow parka over her head, bent her body into the cold squall, and struggled around the corner of the cottage to gather up an armful of wood. A thunderclap rolled through the little valley, and echoed off the surrounding hills. It will be the kind of day, she thought, when a blazing fire and a good book are absolute contentment – although she'd seen no books in the cottage, except for three huge, dog-eared ledgers that leaned against a window recess in the keeping room. Dry reading, that! She thought.

Miss Priss had lovingly and thoroughly washed down and fed her two kittens. There seemed to be no more to come. All three slept blissfully in the box, warmed by the coal stove fire. The tiny dark balls of fluff, tightly locked to their mother's nipples, stood out starkly against her white fur. Grumpkin slept guard nearby, exhausted by her ordeal as watchdog and friend, while the two women settled in their wing chairs before the new fire to meditate.

CRONE; A Meditation on Womanhood

Augusta had noticed that meditating was deeper and more fulfilling with the Crone, because of some undefined but meaningful spirituality imparted simply by her presence.

"Only two kittens," Augusta commented with pleasure. "Priss is ahead of her time, not over-populating the world!" The Crone nodded. "I wonder," Augusta continued, "whether we'll ever teach women to limit their families voluntarily, before we chew the planet to pieces. Women must take all the responsibility, I'm afraid. We have the means, but do we have the will?"

"I pray we do," the Crone replied in a distant, self-absorbed voice.

The two orange cats glided by Augusta's chair. One leaped upon the Crone's lap, kneading the spot intently, balancing precariously on her almost fleshless bones, before finding purchase enough for a secure nap. The other, surprisingly, plunked down next to the overtired puppy and leaned against her fat, heaving tummy, eyes instantly closed in pure satisfaction. It was a day for dozing.

A question had been stirring in the recesses of Augusta's mind, something to do with the deer's behavior last night, and the unusual behavior of the cats just now. Ah, of course, she murmured to herself, it's as if the animals were ignoring my very existence. Where and when have I felt so slighted before? Augusta concentrated her attention on the subtle sensations and memories of her body and mind. Yes, that's it! She recognized the feeling; it had been happening to her more and more often lately – the sensation that she was becoming invisible.

"Mahm!" She jolted the old woman sharply from her reverie. "The strangest thing has been happening for a couple of years now. I used to think something was the matter with me, but now I'm not so sure. I've always been sociable and outgoing, but lately I have the sense – in many different places and situations – that I've become invisible. Do you know what I'm talking about?

"Yes," the Crone answered with a twisted smile. "Older woman -- useless to society. Like it?"

The younger woman contemplated the question. "Truthfully, there was a time when I *didn't* like it. I felt unattractive. Insulted. But lately I see it has an advantage. I can do just about anything I want, and nobody cares. No one even notices. Why, I'm free!" she exclaimed with astonished, mounting pleasure. "No strings at all – just free!" She stared into the fire, conscious of feeling elated, when some movement from the direction of the Crone's chair caught her eye. The wizened old woman was growing in stature, rising toward the ceiling beams, body elongating, taking on an element of mystery, even ferocity. Her eyes sparkled and grew larger, a strange light flowed about her head, and her robe undulated, became aurora borealis. She chanted "Free-dom! Free-dom! FREE-DOM!" with the joyous, insistent beat of a tribal drum. Augusta was terrified. Thunder exploded directly overhead, shaking the house and rattling dishes in the cabinet. Augusta, wrapping both arms over her head, cowered into the corner of her chair. Wham! The door flung open. An imposing white-haired woman threw back the hood of her rain-cape and scattered water in every direction. "What a storm!" she greeted them loudly. "Water on for tea?"

Augusta jerked herself upright.

The Crone was sitting peacefully in her chair, undisturbed and unchanged. "Always, dear," she said, with a noticeable lilt to her voice. "Why are you out in this weather?" Even before they were introduced, Augusta knew this was the Crone's daughter. The inflection in her voice made that clear – the universal, intimate tone of concerned mother. "My daughter Leigh," she said with obvious pride. "Augusta, my guest."

Leigh was tall, far taller than her age-shrunken mother, and had once been athletic, but at seventy-three her body was beginning to diminish – deeply sun-wrinkled face, neck layered with taut folds of skin. "You can always tell a woman's real age by the look of her neck," Augusta's aunt had once told her. She smiled – until cosmetic surgery, anyway.

The two women shook hands with pleasure, looking openly into each other's eyes, without the protection of social masks. And it was even easier, Augusta realized, now that I'm becoming invisible, free to be myself instead of struggling to fill some ill-fitting feminine role, she thought – and a long time coming!

Leigh admired the kittens, and spoke lovingly to Miss Priss, before she and her mother settled into the upholstered chairs. Augusta perched on a low footstool next to the fireplace, leaning against the wall to face the two women, observing one and then the other, so much alike and yet so different – mother silent with wisdom, daughter talkative with experience. The three sipped tea peaceably and chatted on about many things, knowing the subject was unimportant, but the companionship was beyond price.

"Have you become invisible yet?" Leigh asked out of the blue, shocking Augusta so that she almost tumbled off her stool. "I would think you might have."

Recovering herself, Augusta laughed awkwardly. "You two have an uncanny ability to read my mind! And the answer is yes, I have indeed experienced being invisible. Your mother and I were discussing the phenomenon just before you came."

"And are you divorced? That's an even earlier invisibility – an instant social back shelf, so to speak." Leigh continued.

Augusta was more comfortable now, more in tune with this brusque intellect. "So true," she commented, remembering how her fellow church members had instantly ostracized her after her first marriage ended. Not one woman had asked why she'd taken such drastic action, or acknowledged her loneliness or pain. But in those days, divorce simply "wasn't done." After twenty-five years, their insensitivity and judgment still rankled.

Leigh suddenly became quiet, intense. She gave Augusta a piercing look, and said pointedly, "When I was young, my mother sometimes looked to me like an avenging angel ... flaming halo ... rainbow robes .... " She paused expectantly, hopefully.

Augusta glanced toward the Crone, who seemed to be dozing, and then acknowledged the truth of the unspoken question with a quick double-nod, but only said aloud, noncommittally, "Yes, I think I've imagined my mother quite the same way." And with that cryptic interchange, the two women shared much about each other. Augusta was greatly relieved to learn that her observance of the Crone's transformation had been Leigh's experience too, because for a moment she'd seriously questioned her own sanity.

Soon after, the old woman woke, pushed herself up from the wing chair with difficulty, bent on preparing lunch for her guests. She rounded up some bread and butter, a tin of crackers, a large bunch of crisp purple grapes, and a good-sized hunk of soft Brie that had been ripening on the shelf. Augusta fetched the straight-backed chair from the bedroom, and some cider from the spring house crock, delighted to find that the storm had passed as quickly as it had arrived. The mountain air was rapidly warming and promised a sunny, early-summer day.

The benches dried off quickly, and a soft haze rose from the meadow, lifted in gently spinning wisps by a faint breeze and the warming rays of the sun. The three women took to the benches to observe the antics of the geese – feisty males grabbing at each other's necks, wings flailing in hot territorial dispute. Leigh tossed a few grapes to the peacocks, who sprinted up the hill when they recognized their special, benevolent friend.

"The weather's supposed to be marvelous for the Gathering," Leigh commented, "Warm and cloudless. How many are you expecting?" The Crone only shrugged in reply. "I'm guessing well over a hundred," Leigh continued. "Doesn't the word 'Gathering' sound agreeable? I'm not much for parties – too frenetic and exhausting -- but a 'gathering' exudes warmth and friendship, don't you think?" soliciting Augusta's support.

"How often have you had this Gathering?" Augusta wanted to know.

"Oh, this will be the first one. It just grew, somehow, out of some idle remarks about women's work, and summer solstice, and the failing health of Mother Earth. You know, about women's willingness -- even if we don't like the jobs -- to clean, to cook and to care." That phrase again! Augusta was startled, but Leigh smiled at the catchy phrase; her tone had given it positive meaning.

"A gathering of women," she went on, "to reinforce the fact that the action of women will determine how the world will survive in the twenty-first century; how many children we have and how we bring them up; how we spend our money; whether we control our use of fossil fuels and reduce global warming; who we vote for; how we wield our political power. Women are only now grasping the fact that *we are* the significant difference!

"Harness the willingness," said the Crone quietly.

"I'm a retired Sociology professor," Leigh continued, not noticing her mother's profound comment. "Don't I sound like one? I know that men and women don't think in the same ways. Men tend to be merely logical. Wars, and the world's economic decisions, have all been man-made – with our passive approval. Did you know that when little boys play games, they'll battle it out until the rules are clear, until there's a winner and a loser?

"Little girls are basically different. If there's a dispute over rules, and someone gets hurt by the decision, girls instinctively change the game to include everyone. How beautiful that is! It becomes a spiritual game – using 'global' or 'inclusive' thinking – seeing all sides. The kind of attitude that works best in families – and God knows we're a world family now! It's going to take a true global vision to halt runaway consumption, and rescue us from outdated, intolerant, us-against-them thinking!" The last sentence was proclaimed in a strong oratory-voice, as if she were truly on a soapbox. Augusta and the Crone cheered and applauded, and Leigh collapsed into laughter.

"Well, now you know where I stand," she said, a bit out of breath, "and you have the gist of my message for the Gathering. It's bound to be a Happening – lots of friends and singing and candles around the pond. I hope you've ordered enough toilet paper, Mahm."

The Crone nodded. "Don't worry," she said. " Andrea has the list."

CRONE; A Meditation on Womanhood

"That's good. She's so organized! By the way, would you like everyone to repeat your Credo on Womanhood, as a litany? We could print up enough copies to go around."

The Crone nodded enthusiastically. "A keepsake!"

"Okay, I'll print a couple of hundred pocket cards for souvenirs. Well, I'll be going – plenty left to do before then. Better expect people to start coming early in the day, Mahm." She turned to Augusta with the smile of an old friend. "Delightful meeting you, Augusta. See you at the Gathering. My four daughters will be here; they're a bit younger than you are." And with that, she kissed her mother, hugged them both, then strode down the storm-soaked path through sweet-fern and pines, and was soon out of sight, flinging a last jaunty wave toward the sky without even bothering to turn around.

CHAPTER TWELVE

"Nap," pronounced the Crone with a sigh. "I love Leigh, but she exhausts me." The ancient woman moved with painful slowness up the cottage stairs. Augusta washed the few dishes before following her.

"I'm not at all tired or sleepy, Mahm," she said to the old woman, who was already snuggled comfortably into her pillow. "I'd love to read something peaceful, but I haven't seen a book in the house."

"Ledgers," the Crone responded in a drowsy voice.

Augusta, silently wondering what inspiration the ledgers held, returned to the keeping room and withdrew the oldest leather-bound volume from its resting place. She was surprised by the intensity of her anticipation, prolonging the moment by caressing the battered, brick-red leather with her fingers,

CRONE; A Meditation on Womanhood

instinctively knowing that a revelation awaited her inside. History? Biography? Mystery?

The thick cover opened easily to the first page, revealing the Crone's young handwriting, faded ink on paper with age-browned edges:

Being a Book of Spiritual Gifts

She turned the page eagerly, and saw the same strong, old-fashioned script:

December 21, 1935 - The stone cottage has just received a blanket of new snow, and some generous, unknown soul has shoveled the whole path while I slept. The final touch is a handmade spray of holly, ivy and evergreen boughs hanging on the front door. What a glorious gift to greet the Christmas season! I never feel alone in this blessed cottage.

"The very year I was born, Augusta noted with some surprise. She read on. An entirely different hand-writing:

December 22. My Christmas gift to you and our common Spirit, dear lady, is a year of volunteer work at the city mission. I wash dishes and make beds - a new skill for an old lawyer!
-- Theodore

She was astounded by her discovery. The Crone had been living in the cottage for as long as Augusta had been on this earth, but her home hadn't collected a clutter of merely material things.

No, indeed. She had been collecting only actions, the memories of spiritual gifts, acts of loving kindness, good works – deeds immortalized by the words in these vibrant ledgers!

December 24 (another handwriting) I have answered letters to Santa Claus for two weeks at the post office. I've cried a bucket of tears! Emma

December 25. Merry Christmas! I drive an elderly woman to the market each week, and carry her groceries. I shop for her when the weather is bad, and I only hope someone will be around to do the same for me some day. Jane

Augusta continued to read, with ever-increasing fascination, convinced that she was spying on the most personal and private behaviors of thoughtful people. These were simple, everyday acts of kindness, not unusual or earth-shaking, and yet, because they were offered to the Crone in lieu of material gifts, the very acts became a consecration. She could almost hear her ancient hostess now. "What have you been doing, my dear? Write it down for me to remember."

April 4, 1937. I got Betty's cat down. She cry. Tim

(Was it the cat who cried, or Betty? Augusta wondered.)

March 10, 1942. I volunteer at the Veteran's hospital, reading to the men who have been blinded in the war. They tell me they're glad I come every week. It's very hard for me to go there, but I never miss a day. That would be too cruel. Eloise

November 20, 1944. I cleaned the gutters for the old people's home this weekend. Nathan.

July 7, 1947. I made cookies for Grandma. They did not burn. Not one. Marianne

More than an hour had passed, and she had not even reached 1950. Augusta was so engrossed that she heard nothing else, saw nothing else but these precious, mundane gifts of simple humanity, filled with love and, all too often, underlying heartache. Recorded by ordinary people, children and adults alike, they tumbled forth year upon year, some rambling on for a page or more and others, like Tim's, so sparse as to leave the reader wondering about the full story.

Augusta was quite overwhelmed by the emotional out-pouring. It brought to mind a modern parable so poignant that she had never been able to repeat it aloud without emotion:

> "There is but one major difference between hell and heaven. In the one, a magnificent dining table has been spread with every imaginable food, forever fresh, delectable and inviting, tantalizing aromas streaming forth to thrill the appetites of the guests. But they are unable to eat, because one hand is tied behind their backs, and the other is bound to a spoon whose handle is too long to reach their drooling mouths. The room is alive with groans of self-pity and frustration.
>
> In the other chamber, the food is equally sumptuous and the circumstances identical, but the attitude of the dinner guests is very different; with uncommon regard and genuine respect, they take turns feeding one another."
> (Author unknown)

Augusta sat for some time, eyes closed, visualizing the constant flow of pilgrims up the long mountain path to the stone cottage, looking for companionship or solace, seeking to heal their spirits with a nod of total acceptance. Suddenly curious about the newest writings, she reached for the third and most recent ledger, less worn and frayed than the other two. She turned to the last entry, only 3 pages from the end of the book.

June 19. Thank you for giving me the gift of myself. I had some tough decisions to make, and I wanted you to decide for me. Thanks for just listening instead. **Andrea**

The cottage's guest felt as if she'd entered an inner sanctum, and unveiled a world far grander than anything she had imagined. How could this be? Helping a friend or stranger is as old as humankind, and just as natural. And yet, for Augusta, the ledgers had the immediacy and intensity of revealed truth. For the moment, she felt filled to overflowing with the richness of this feast.

Soft shuffling sounds above stairs alerted her that the Crone had wakened. Augusta hurriedly shoveled a scoop of coal into the stove, and added kindling, noticing how tiny the barely glowing pile of embers had become; she slid the teakettle onto the round, black stove-lid, to get the full benefit of the new blaze, and peeked into Priss's box. A contented mother half-opened her eyes, and seemed to smile at this morning's midwife, while the two kittens nuzzled busily, tiny paws star-fished on their mother's belly.

The Crone walked cautiously, hesitantly around the cottage, following the path from the outhouse to the front door. She clutched a sturdy walking staff, pausing every so often to look around her at the beauty of her homestead, each view a memorized picture of wonder and charm, from hazy-purple mountains to shimmering pond, to yellow-green meadow, to shadow-dark pines silhouetted against the sky. Grumpkin bounced beside her. Reaching the bench at last, she leaned on it with both hands, lowering her body gingerly to the plank seat. Although she disregarded them whenever possible, the aches of advanced age had not ignored her; they came and went with whim and weather.

Augusta appeared with a mug of tea; the Crone accepted, inhaling the fragrant vapors gratefully, as the two women admired the serene little valley, wanting for nothing.

"I've read some of your gifts, Mahm," Augusta acknowledged at last. "I have no words! It's a revelation to read them – as if I'd stepped unexpectedly into Esse's private chambers."

The Crone glanced over at her with a soft, benign look in her eyes, and nodded several times. "Ripple of blessings, " she assented.

"Do you especially look forward to holidays," Augusta went on, "because you know your friends will be adding to your book?"

"Oh. No," replied the Crone. "Always with me." And with that last, satisfied comment, the two closed their eyes for their afternoon meditation, undisturbed by peacocks screaming in the distance, the raucous complaints of geese, and the yipping of Grumpkin as she bounded joyously away down the hill.

CHAPTER THIRTEEN

Opening their eyes minutes later, they were surprised to discover a young woman seated on the ground, her back against the big boulder, her lap overflowing with sleeping puppy. She looked from one woman to the other and smiled serenely; hers was the face of a Renaissance angel – a strong, commanding beauty. Most assuredly she was one of the Crone's relatives: contours reminiscent of a young Leigh were repeated in her profile and deep-set eyes.

The Crone's face had taken on a beatific glow. "My great-granddaughter Faith," she introduced the young woman. Augusta saw that her ancient hostess regarded this child with extraordinary affection, expressed through the renewed light in her eyes and the unexpected lilt to her aged voice. And that love was obviously returned in equal measure.

"Hi," said the young angel, just as any ordinary person would. The middle-aged matron was instantly reminded of her own beautiful daughter, so spiritually alive and in tune with the present. Augusta felt a split-second pang of regret for her own generation's inability to give up outdated roles, and envy of this new generation's willingness to deal with life on its own terms, with fewer of yesterday's self-imposed limitations.

"I'd get up," Faith went on, "but ..." she gestured helplessly toward Grumpkin, who was clearly not willing to relinquish this lap of honor. "Has Priss had her kittens yet?" she asked expectantly.

"Two. This morning," the Crone replied with unusual satisfaction.

"Oh, Mahm," Faith exclaimed. "Two? She must've somehow gotten your message about the population explosion!" She laughed so hard that the puppy was shaken awake, rolling from Faith's lap onto the ground with a thump. "I must see them!" The young woman hugged her great-grandmother enthusiastically, and hurried into the cottage, where she could be heard murmuring admiringly to the mother.

Augusta looked quizzically at the old woman.

"My favorite great-grand," the Crone answered her look. "She'll live here one day." And with that simple yet all-encompassing declaration, this woman of wisdom had proclaimed Faith to be the heir .... to what? Eventually to the homestead, yes, but Augusta knew it implied worlds more: a way of thinking, a manner of being, an understanding of personal responsibility, a reverence for Esse within herself and in all things. It was a blessing plaited with heartache and agony, but she was certain this young woman would be ready when the time came – not because of what she could do, but who she was becoming.

"My mother's name was Faith," she said to the young woman on her return to the benches. "I think she disliked it because it was so old-fashioned, but to me it had the ring of rightness, so it's also my own daughter's middle name."

Faith settled cross-legged on the grass, and looked contentedly at the distant mountains. "It's quite a name to live up to, actually," she replied at last. "and I certainly haven't grown into it yet."

I've brought a friend with me for the weekend, Mahm," she continued, changing the subject. "Her name's Maddie. She's down with the horses right now. We brought a coupla sleeping bags, and I thought we could sleep at the Seat – if no one's in line before us."

"Good," the Crone replied with obvious pleasure, and indeed they could see Maddie now, petting Liberty at the fence. They all beckoned to her, and she immediately started for the cottage, stopping every so often to admire the view, the pond, the animals. Everyone knows instinctively that it's okay not to stand on ceremony here, Augusta thought to herself. Maddie seemed especially taken with the peacocks, who had been silent for awhile, and now began their territorial screaming, as if they'd only just remembered their purpose in life.

"What do you do?" Augusta asked Faith.

"Oh, I'm a Social Worker," came the reply. "Anne's got serious family problems, and I thought a weekend with some strong, motivated women would do her good. By the way, we're making dinner tonight. I brought enough food for a whole summer camp!"

The Crone smiled warmly. "Come," she urged, patting the bench beside her. "Where is Caroline?"

"Aunt Sophie's bringing her later," Faith explained.

"Good!" The Crone responded with satisfaction. The women continued to chat comfortably until Maddie arrived and was introduced around. A frightened young woman with large, dark eyes and a hesitant smile, clearly depressed and preoccupied, stood before them. She tried to make herself less visible by constantly averting her eyes. Faith soon pulled her away for a hike up to the seat, so they could stow their sleeping bags and lay a campfire – promising to begin supper as soon as they returned.

* * *

The two young women bustled about the keeping room, while Augusta and the Crone waited – impatiently and patiently – for supper. Maddie was a big-city girl who had never so much as imagined water pumps, coal stoves and springhouses. As she tried to follow Faith's rapid-fire instructions, she was obviously in culture shock, racing to and from the springhouse, losing the prime on the water pump, burning her hand on the stove, dropping firewood on her foot.

Augusta looked on with amusement, realizing that Faith's technique was having the desired effect. The effort to prepare a simple meal in these primitive conditions had already ignited a spark in Maddie's eyes rivaling the candle flame.

At last the two young friends dragged the smaller bench into the keeping room, and pronounced, "*Mesdames sont servies*," in their most butlery manner, arms linked together, bowing from the waist, folded towels draped upon their arms. Augusta offered her crooked elbow to the Crone, and they paraded inside as if to a banquet.

The flickering fire, and the light from candles atop two ancient brass candlesticks, threw soft shadows into every corner of the room, lending a subtle glow to the serving dishes on the small table – tossed green salad, eggplant casserole still bubbling from the oven, warm sour-milk biscuits and butter, spiced watermelon rind, and mugs of cold cranberry juice.

CRONE; A Meditation on Womanhood

The four women seated themselves and held hands for Faith's blessing:

> "Thank you, Esse, for this day filled with your gifts of life and love. We are grateful for the lives of the women seated at this bountiful table. Bless us all – especially my wonderful Mahm. Amen."

Faith squeezed the Crone's hand lightly, points of candlelight gleaming at the corners of her eyes. Augusta savored the contentment on their faces, the plaintive mewing of the kittens in their box, the sound of a few peepers at the pond trilling their spring mating song. After supper, the two older women ensconced themselves by the fireplace, while the new guests handled the domestic chores – heating wash water, scrubbing pots, wiping down the table, drying the few dishes and returning them to their cabinet home.

Maddie hustled about in a haze of amazement. Imagine not having hot running water, a dishwasher, electricity! Augusta was fascinated by Faith's treatment of the young woman. She deftly directed each procedure, and praised Maddie's work in subtle, supportive ways. In fact, Faith did little of the cleanup herself, but soon, under her thoughtful tutelage, Maddie was moving with greater confidence. They dried their hands on the dishtowels, giggling and mopping their brows in mock relief over hard work accomplished.

"How about an armful of firewood, Maddie," Faith said, as if the city woman routinely foraged into the sinister mountain night. Fear flashed across her face, but Maddie hesitated only a moment before stepping into the crisp air. The woodpile against the wall was just visible in the pale light from the kerosene lamp that Faith hurried to place in the window.

Augusta took the opportunity to praise Faith's skillful work. "Well done," she said, needing to explain herself no further. "Thanks," Faith replied. "I'm trying to give her a lot in a very short time."

CRONE; A Meditation on Womanhood

"I know. I've been a counselor myself for twenty years. It is a joy for me to see some defeated person come alive, and ..." (Here, Augusta searched for the right word, gesturing expansively) "... blossom with new hope."

"Oh yes!" Faith exclaimed fervently. "It thrills me too!" And they found themselves nodding in shared commitment and passion, knowing that helping someone discover herself is a true gift. "Tonight at the Seat will be such fun!" They both grinned, imagining it.

"Hasn't Maddie been gone a long time?" Faith suddenly noticed. She hurried to the door, only to discover her friend sitting on the bench, firewood gathered beside her, staring off toward the pond in a deep reverie. "Maddie!" she exclaimed. "Are you okay?"

Maddie looked at her calmly. "Just fine," she replied with unruffled assurance, "enjoying the moonlight." Faith joined her on the bench, wrapping her arms around herself to fend off the chill.

"It's so peaceful here," Maddie continued. "I just realized that I don't have to be afraid, if I don't want to be. Isn't that amazing? I came outside so terrified that I could hardly breathe, and then the geese started to squawk – and it struck me. Oh, Faith, thanks for bringing me here. I needed this so much!" And she gave her friend a quick hug.

They shivered in the chill, moonlit air, caught in wonder as they gazed at millions of brilliantly sharp star-points in a black velvet sky. "I never knew there were so many stars, or so bright!" the city girl cried. "I could stay here forever!"

The moon's reflection on the placid pond was softly polished silver, until the surface suddenly erupted in a turmoil of shattered moonlight, water whipped to boiling froth by some underwater demon. "*What's happening?*" Maddie exclaimed.

"Fish in a mating frenzy, Faith explained. They're just as much in love with moonlight as people are – maybe more so!"

Their infectious laughter preceded them into the warm cottage. Augusta and the Crone caught it and tossed it between them. They could see that Maddie had truly been transformed. Her body was now straight and tall, her head high, eyes eager to connect, a sure symptom of her new sense of self-worth. Faith and Augusta passed conspiratorial glances. "It's what we're here for," they acknowledged silently, and Augusta realized that no generation gap whatsoever separated them. Had it been bridged? No, she decided; it had simply never existed.

Maddie fed the fire enthusiastically, shifting logs with an iron poker, then seated herself on one of the footstools flanking the fireplace, while Faith perched on the other, facing the older women. The newest guest was the first to speak. "I needed to be here," she said. "I've been struggling with a terrible problem. The time away and this place have already given me some strength."

"Do you want to tell us about it?" Augusta asked quietly.

Maddie looked at her hands, turning them to and fro, examining the nails, twisting a gold ring. "I have a beautiful little girl, five years old," she answered at last, almost in a whisper. "Her name is Leta." Maddie became silent again, her inner turmoil evident to her listeners.

"She's staying with my mother right now because, lately, something's been very wrong at home. She doesn't say much, but she doesn't want me to go out and leave her alone with Daddy. The strange thing is, when he *does* baby-sit for her, she runs and hugs him as if she's thrilled. Oh, I can't explain it. But it seems like a new person takes over inside her. Faith suggested that we both see a counselor." She sighed heavily. The women were still, only the crackle of the fire breaking the silence of the room.

"My husband is such a straight arrow. Sometimes I'm afraid I must be imagining things!" Maddie swallowed with difficulty before continuing. "Incest" (she had finally said the word aloud) "is such a strong taboo. I can't believe my Jimmie would ever do something so horrible. He idolizes her." Maddie sank back against the wall, eyes squeezed tightly shut, looking smaller – as if something had begun to seep out of her. Augusta prayed it would bring her some relief.

The Crone pulled herself upright in her chair. "Incest is not a taboo!" she said in a voice that crackled with power. The words were like an exploding grenade; the women recoiled, mouths opened involuntarily, eyes widened with shock. Maddie's face froze; her skin paled and became instantly damp. Faith, after that first stunning blow, sat quietly, allowing the full impact of the message to settle into her. Augusta's mind reacted in slow motion, until she was able to refocus and return to reality – and the raw truth of the Crone's statement changed her perception forever.

"Incest is all too common to be labeled a taboo," Faith continued her great-grandmother's thought, "and the damage colors a little girl's whole life. I don't mean to leave out little boys; they're abused too, but not in such overwhelming numbers. She gazed intently at each woman in turn. "The true taboo seems to be against women warning their children of possible dangers as a matter of course. Our loyalties get strained here, as you can imagine. The real question is, who owns our body – beginning as a baby? Who's responsible? Will we really talk about these things together? Share our experiences and fears with other women?

"We should be loyal to our innocent children *first*, but traditionally we're loyal to our man – financially and emotionally –- so denial takes over. When incest breaks family unity, we tend to react with shame; telling the truth may well break up the family unit, so... on some level we sacrifice the little child instead. How hideous!" Faith, her face a mask of revulsion and pain, took a long breath.

"And it's women who make that final decision – consciously or unconsciously. But we can't fix something we won't discuss! We're just scratching the surface, now that so many women are speaking to the hard truth – but we have a long, long way to go!"

Maddie had dropped her head into her cradled arms and was rocking back and forth in agony. "It's all my fault," came her muffled voice.

"Ah, no, Maddie," Augusta broke into her distress. "You've begun to talk about it just as soon as you could. It takes real courage to leave all our passive, good-girl upbringing behind us. I have to remember that I was thirty-five before I made my very first

68

decision – that is, one that I made just for *me*, not based on social pressure. That's when I got a divorce."

Something in the older woman's voice made Maddie raise her head. She saw compassion and understanding in Augusta's eyes. No further conversation passed between them, and indeed very little needed to be said. All four women hugged one another, knowing that some powerful bond had been forged among them. Then the Crone rummaged in the closet for a flashlight, and the two young women departed for their starlit bedroom, up the path beyond the outhouse.

CHAPTER FOURTEEN

Augusta was awake long before sunrise. She dressed quietly, hurriedly, noticing that the Crone didn't stir, despite the little noises she was making. Grumpkin lifted her head sleepily, but lowered it again onto her paws, once she realized that the wrong person was getting up.

Augusta pulled a shawl down from the peg by the door, and wrapped the coarse, thick wool tightly around her shoulders with one hand as, flashlight in the other, she followed the path to the outhouse. The chill cut through her clothes, and she wondered how Faith and Maddie were surviving in their open sleeping quarters. What an experience for someone who had known only the steep, straight canyons of the city!

Returning to the cottage, she half-slid down the side path to the front door, startled by the sudden crowing of the cock in this world of grays. The stars were fading, she noticed, and the mountain's ridge line was defining itself against the barely lighter sky. Augusta sat down on the bench, feeling the haze of cold dew on old wood. The homestead was at peace. Even the geese had

CRONE; A Meditation on Womanhood

failed to take note of her presence, although she could just make out a close grouping of white blotches, where the pond's surface would soon be visible.

Mountain dawn contains none of the theatrical drama of sunrise on the ocean, where that first blue-white flash speeds across the waves like a laser beam to the eyes. Nonetheless, Augusta had a strong urge to welcome this first light. She sat motionless. The blanket of black imperceptibly became gray, became shadows, became shapes, became the silhouette of sweet fern and pine. All at once, Earth came alive. The geese awoke as a single, complaining battalion, and the peacocks screamed "Help! Help! Help!" Augusta was always delighted by the humor of it: such a horrid sound issuing from such a regal bird.

But the early light was rapidly muted and then suppressed by a series of somber clouds that reached above the pines and stretched long fingers toward the cottage, lengthening and expanding as they came, borne forward by a lofty wind. Augusta watched with mounting uneasiness as the cloud-fingers merged into one menacing hand that re-shrouded the valley in pre-dawn gloom.

She was dismayed by her sense of foreboding. The dark cloud pattern seemed to embody the very hand of death. Augusta stood spellbound for a long moment, failing to notice the open cottage door, until the puppy bounced against her leg in frantic welcome mixed with a desperate need to relieve herself after a long sleep. The Crone silently observed the spectacle from the doorway.

"Oh, Mahm!" Augusta exclaimed, with fear in her voice. "What do you make of it?" The old woman only shrugged, perhaps unwilling to share her perception aloud. She dropped heavily onto the bench, and reached for Augusta's hand, as if to minimize the menace of the greater hand poised over the homestead.

All the while the two women watched, the sun was rising inexorably behind the strange cloud, eventually touching its dismal-dark edges with the slimmest trim of silver. A gust of wind cleansed the center into nebulous mist, and the sun broke through – beams of light radiating in a blossoming sunburst, as if the

CRONE; A Meditation on Womanhood

gigantic hand were holding the soaring spirit of life itself in its palm.

For some little time, Faith and Maddie had been standing mesmerized on the path. They had seen everything – felt everything. Instinctively, Augusta rose to join them, and the three drew close together, arms wrapped around each other's waists, breathing sighs of relief as the dawning sun swept away their fear. The Crone remained separate from the others, alone and seemingly untouched.

The ominous cloud dispersed as rapidly as it had come, drifting away over the hill behind the cottage. The full face of the sun flooded the valley with lemon-yellow light, promising azure sky and a sweater-free evening.

Faith hurried inside to heat up water for tea, while Augusta joined the Crone on the bench. "Now, Mahm," she said with returning calm, "please tell me what that was all about."

The older woman answered in her usual laconic manner, with a gentle smile of contentment. "Spirit lives forever."

Augusta inhaled sharply, trying to hide her irritation at the Crone's simplistic answer. At the very least, she had expected the old woman to acknowledge the apparent symbolism of death, or the nameless fear, or the mysterious meaning of the omen, yet she had moved far beyond that. Augusta's foreboding had been sidestepped, and she was left with nothing but unadorned hope. Ah well, she thought, as she gazed out across the pond, welcoming an unexpected tranquility that wrapped itself about her – perhaps it was enough.

CHAPTER FIFTEEN

"That was truly terrifying!" Maddie said through a mouthful of English muffin and raspberry jam. "I thought it was the end of the world sure enough!" The four women, seated around the kitchen table in front of bowls heaped with bananas and white grapes, recalled the menacing hand, and tried to make sense of it. Only the Crone was untouched, her age and attitude separating her from their melodramatic musings.

"I can't help wondering: is it a warning of some kind?" Faith commented, as she took another spoonful of fruit.

"Mahm thinks it's a simple message," Augusta felt moved to explain. "Spirit lives forever. And Spirit overcomes death and darkness too. Is that right, Mahm?" The ancient woman nodded as her thin fingers, evidencing only the slightest tremor of age, picked absently at a piece of muffin.

"Well, I've never seen anything like it in all my years on the mountain," Faith added. "But, in the end, the way the hand caught the brilliance of the sun in its palm gave me such hope." With that, she began to clear the table. "When will everyone start coming to your birthday party, Mahm?" she deftly changed the subject. The Crone's head jerked up, birdlike, and she frowned , causing Faith to correct her words instantly. "Sorry, I mean the Gathering."

"Tents this morning," the Crone answered cryptically, as she headed outside for her morning meditation on her sun-warmed bench.

"Whoa, I'm confused!" Augusta exclaimed. "I thought the Gathering was just a celebration of the summer solstice."

Faith shook her head with a laugh. "It's much more than that. Tomorrow morning, everyone will be on the hillside below the horse barn to welcome the sun. Maybe a coupla hundred people. The village has been doing that for years – they even set up portable toilets. But tomorrow is also Mahm's ninetieth. She disapproves of birthdays. She thinks every day should celebrate the gift of birth. And there's some point to that, don't you think?

CRONE; A Meditation on Womanhood

72

But this time we decided to honor her in a special way. Tonight all her woman friends are coming with candles, and a lot of them will be camping in the meadow. You won't believe it, but she's insisting that we serve only carrot cake and spring water. Tomorrow it'll be just her family.

"Oh, yes, I'd believe it!" Augusta said, obviously referring to the cake. "I'm so glad I'm here. She's a vital part of my life already – the uncanny way she can get to the heart of things with so few words. I've done more soul-searching in these few days than in the whole past year!" She sat very still, staring out the window at the sparkling pond.

"Yes, she has that power with everyone she touches," Faith agreed. "I like to call her Great-Grandma Guru, but that embarrasses her. Hey, let's get this bench outside," she went on, lifting one end of it, "and join her morning meditation. I've been teaching Maddie about listening to life, and I told her this is the very best place to practice."

The Crone had been waiting for her guests and, as they joined her, she lifted a thin-fingered hand that seemed a combined greeting and benediction. The four women sat together comfortably, observing the amiable movements of the homestead's animals as they went about their daily business. Miss Priss sauntered by, searching out the brightest rays of the warming sun for a few minutes' respite from her babies. She, too, closed her eyes to meditate (as cats are wont to do), even as the cacophony of life persisted undiminished around them.

Within a half-hour, the women were chatting again over cups of lemon grass tea. "How was your night out under the stars," Augusta asked Maddie.

"It was spectacular!" she answered enthusiastically. "The stars were *huge*. And so *cold!* Faith made a little campfire, and a herd of deer walked right by us after the flames had gone out. She said the weren't afraid of us 'cuz we're vegetarian. Isn't that neat?"

Maddie continued to ramble on about the excitement of her evening. Then she said, "Faith told a story about herself. When she was ten, she stayed here in the spring – agreeing to go to bed

CRONE; A Meditation on Womanhood

when the whippoorwill called. The funny thing is, it always calls at sunset, but she didn't know that. So she got to stay up a little later every night, and her grandmother felt honor-bound to abide by the original agreement." They chuckled at Faith's good luck, recalling how difficult it is, especially when you're young, to cope with all the surprises and twists of this life, and to maintain integrity when the rules seem to change every day.

Maddie continued to think back over the evening. "And we talked a lot about teaching our little girls how to improve their self-worth. You can explain it better than I can, Faith."

The Crone's great-granddaughter shifted to the big rock, so that she could face her audience of three. "We were discussing little Leta's situation, how she tried her damnedest, only five years old, to tell her mother something was wrong, by saying "no!" in the best way she could. Like most parents, Maddie thought she was just being rebellious and ornery, and made her stick to the rules they had set up – stay with your father, do what you're told, don't say no to your parents, adult plans are more important – that kinda stuff."

Leigh had approached along the path, a large brown envelope in her hand. She stood quietly by as Faith spoke, not wanting to interrupt. Then she sat down next to her granddaughter, gave her a huge hug, and looked for a long, long moment with absolute delight into her face. Faith threw her arms around the old woman's neck. "You always smell so good, Gramma," she cried, as if it were an age-old ritual greeting, which indeed it was.

"Go on, dear. What you're saying is important," Leigh urged her.

Faith looked from one absorbed face to the next. "And then we wondered what would happen if we actually honored every 'no' when a child said it, and learned the reason for every negative attitude by *really* listening, before making a decision.

"You mean, act as if children are real people instead of objects to push around?" Augusta exclaimed with mock astonishment. "Why, that was practically unheard of in my time.

What if they say 'No' to spinach and bedtime? 'No' to raincoats and boots? It would be utter chaos!"

Then Augusta dropped her mockery and continued in a more serious tone. "It probably *would* be chaotic for a while, but if children know they'll always be listened to, perhaps they won't have to rebel against foolish things. If every person's innermost spirit is pure, then refusing to accept a child's 'No!' is negating her true spirit, isn't it? When I finally discovered I could *choose* to say 'no,' my self-esteem sky-rocketed."

Maddie jumped in. "I've been so thoroughly trained to be a good girl, that I actually feel sick with guilt when I say 'no' to *any*thing, even when I'm sure it will be bad for me to say 'yes'!"

Faith nodded. "Allowing ourselves true freedom takes a lot of effort. It's new territory. Most women were taught as children to ignore their own wishes – and so it goes on from generation to generation."

The Crone, who had been listening intently, inhaled one deep, rasping breath, which caused everyone to pay heed. "She *only* wanted attention," she quoted, in a voice of strong conviction mixed with heavy sadness.

"Oh, yes, that always makes my stomach churn!" Augusta exclaimed. "Wanting attention is crying out for love. I hate it when someone says disparagingly, 'she just wants attention.' Don't we all? Why can't we spend a few minutes and just *give* it? If all children were given that attention – that love – whenever they craved it, I wonder where this world would be right now." Augusta ceased speaking, but her outrage kept grew -- even as she noticed that the Crone had dozed off, and her head was bobbing as she breathed, as if she agreed with Augusta's premise.

"Funny you're on this subject, Leigh said, holding up the large, overstuffed envelope. "I've just finished the workshop outline that Mahm and I designed. I'll be passing out copies this evening. The parenting workshops are all on this subject – showing a mother how to hear a true 'No' and respect it, without just reacting."

CRONE; A Meditation on Womanhood

"Whew!" Augusta was finally able to blow away her anger. "I'd like to see a copy of that. Get rid of all that old sin-based you're-always-wrong thinking and allow personal integrity to grow, right from day one!" The other women, totally engrossed in the conversation, were vigorously nodding their heads.

Leigh looked at her closely. "What's your special talent?"

The middle-aged woman was surprised by the quick change of subject. "Oh, I do several things. Addictions counselor, some writing ..."

"What kind of writing?" came the instantly eager reply.

"Mostly books on addictions and personal growth." Augusta answered the Crone's daughter, noticing the conspiratorial glances that passed between Leigh and Faith. "What do you have in mind?" she asked suspiciously.

"Perhaps you're here on a special mission," Leigh explained. "We need a writer to tell the Crone's story. It needs to be from an objective eye. Yours is the talent we've been missing up to now."

"Perhaps," Augusta replied. "I'm convinced I'm here for a definite purpose, and I'd like to spend some time later talking about it with you. But now, please explain why you called your mother 'Crone.' It's a word that's flashed through my head a lot, this past couple of days."

Leigh laughed. "Of course it has. Everyone thinks of her as 'The Crone of the Mountain.' The original meaning is the old ewe in a flock of sheep. For us, she's the ancient wise woman who passes her wisdom and knowledge on to the next generation."

Augusta laughed along with her. "I've heard that 'to crone' means to *remove* the ancient ewe from the flock. For mutton, I suppose. Perhaps, like old women, old ewes finally discover they're free to think for themselves. Maybe they get feisty and obstreperous and disturb the passive flock."

Leigh burst in to laughter. "Oh, that's my mother, all right!" she exclaimed. For fifty years she's been poking at the status quo, proclaiming as fact what a great many of us are now just coming to believe – but she's a true visionary, decades ahead of her time."

CRONE; A Meditation on Womanhood

$\mathcal{A}$NTICIPATION

$\mathcal{C}$HAPTER SIXTEEN

Just beyond hearing of the cottage guests, a bustle of activity was taking place. In the past hour, numerous tents had sprung up like overnight toadstools, in a variety of marvelous shapes and colors. The lower meadow was filling fast. A few vans had been parked neatly, facing the edge of the woods, as if some organizing influence was managing the growing throng. Augusta guessed that Andrea was somehow involved in every facet of the operation.

Drawn by curiosity, the two older women followed Maddie and Faith around the pond, Augusta curbing her step to Leigh's naturally slower pace. The trail that Jenny and Linda had traveled yesterday curved past the barn and paddock, skirted an outcropping of shale, and meandered downhill into the next meadow, ending at the edge of the county road. A clear spring bubbled up at the base of the rock outcropping, into a pool encircled by flat shale shards, interspersed with tufts of lush spring grasses. Two women, one with a month-old baby in a breast sling, were filling water bottles.

As soon as the four passed these rocks, they entered an entirely different world of high energy. Faith hurried on ahead, and was quickly surrounded by welcoming arms and shouts of joyful reunion. She seemed to know everyone. "Maddie, come over here," she called, introducing her to childhood acquaintances from the village. Another van pulled up, letting out a team of four laughing girls with badminton racquets.

Leigh had promised a "happening," and Augusta could see it had already become one. Twin sisters in pale blue cut-offs raced across the meadow, loosening their hold on matching kites that lifted rapidly above the campers heads amid cheers and shouts and several long whistles. Arms outstretched, the new kite experts squatted together on the grass, gazing proudly at the shrinking airborne specks, while a younger child in pigtails mimicked their every move, raised arms controlling her own phantom kite.

Leaving Leigh near the spring to chat with old friends, Augusta wandered through another grassy meadow that was fast becoming an orderly campground of tents and folding chairs. As promised, several portable toilets had been delivered to the site, tucked discreetly under some shade trees near the road. And yes, there was Andrea, long black hair swinging, directing traffic just as Augusta had suspected. They waved to each other, signaling with an upraised finger that she wanted Augusta to wait a moment.

Augusta strolled slowly through the temporary village, smiling and greeting the residents she passed. Four frosty-haired women had arranged their camp chairs in a semicircle under a broad, shady swamp-maple, where they had a panoramic view of the activities.

"Is the Crone having visitors?" one of them called out to her. "Oh, yes, I'm sure she is," Augusta replied. "Why don't you go up to the cottage now, before she takes her nap?" She watched the four as they greeted Leigh with loving hugs, then wended their way slowly past the spring, stopping often, a little out of breath on the gentle slope, but determined to reach the cottage.

Augusta now understood something of the geography of the homestead. She had come to the cottage from the north, by way of a high mountain footpath that veered away to the right, off the county road. That graveled asphalt ribbon then wound through the valley to the village of Miraton, which lay on the far side of the mountain. She was relieved to discover a broad, sandy, roadside parking area; finding the homestead a second time would be far simpler and less mysterious.

What an unusual gathering of people, Augusta decided, continuing her walk through the meadow. Three peculiarities especially intrigued her. First, wherever she turned, only females met her eye – little girls, teen-age girls, young, middle-aged and old women, and several certified crones who moved with deliberate concentration. The broad spectrum of age fascinated her, because she had seldom been part of a group spanning several generations, except perhaps a family reunion. Ah, but wasn't the Crone's birthday just that: a gathering of family, of emotional, philosophical and blood kin all come to honor their matriarch?

Secondly, she was discovering a group more eclectic than she would ever have imagined. These women arrived with or without makeup, in slacks or jeans, in vans and sports cars. She would soon learn that they were married, divorced and single; gay and straight; and of every social class, color and culture, reflecting the deeply spiritual character of the Crone, who had openly loved and accepted so many women over such a long span of years.

But it was the third oddity that truly piqued Augusta's curiosity. Each person, large or small, wore a mug at her waist; some were painted tin, but most were ceramic; some were tied with a bandanna through the handle, others fastened with a clip or macramé thong. Still others had been fashioned with a sizable hole near the lip, which cleverly avoided the problem of weak handles. The mugs themselves were magnificent creations of glinting glazes and bright colors, with personal names or serious messages like "Save the World," and "Pro-choice." Designs were limited only by the dreams of the artist.

Augusta was finally able to ask Andrea about the fashion. "Hardly a fad," came the quick reply. "Everyone in Miraton wears a mug. It's an ecology-minded town, so just about everything gets recycled. Our supermarket's been discouraging extra packaging

CRONE: A Meditation on Womanhood

and plastic bags for years. Our fast-food restaurant has a low-fat menu. What a great place to live -- a true miracle town. That's why we named it Miraton. I hope you'll visit some day soon."

As she described the village, Andrea was actually glowing with pride, Augusta realized. "It's more than sixty percent female, and most of the politicians are women. I think that's what makes the real difference. They're less into power for its own sake than men are, and more in touch with protecting Mother Earth. Besides, women decide how to spend most of the household money anyway, so we can really control what we consume, like cars and clothes and cleaning products, if we care enough. It all begins with example and education."

"But about the mugs. One of the pottery teachers is a longtime member of Alcoholics Anonymous. She figured that, nationwide, they toss out millions of Styrofoam cups every single night. She made personalized mugs for her whole group that year, asking people to use them at every meeting, instead of Styrofoam or paper. The idea caught on. Then she got her seventh graders to design their own – and the idea kept spreading. It was once the "in" thing to wear a mug, but I don't think that's true any more. For the younger generation, it's just the way we do things in Miraton."

"I wanted you to have a souvenir," Andrea continued, untying a purple batik bandanna at her waist. "I made it myself just this year." From the soft cloth dangled a hand-thrown, handle-less mug. Augusta, hunting hurriedly for her glasses, accepted the gift, turning it in both hands as slowly and reverently as a chalice. The glazes depicted a primitive gray stone cottage, a blue pond, and a peacock, whose long tail encircled the base.

She was too moved to speak. Avoiding the emotion of the moment, she ducked her head to tie the gift to her own belt. It was a strangely satisfying sensation, that gentle weight against her hip. Then the two women gave each other a quick, hard hug. Augusta blinked rapidly to dash away her tears. "Thank you," she whispered at last.

CHAPTER SEVENTEEN

Andrea had an immediate mission. "Will you come help me?" She asked Augusta.

The other woman, glad to be of service, soon found herself pulling a well-balanced, two-wheeled garden cart, as Andrea pushed from behind. A towering load of boxes clinked with the sound of knocking glass. The cart and its contents rolled past the spring, and up the incline to a natural sandpit near the barn. "What are we going to do?" Augusta asked in bewilderment.

"You'll see," the young woman answered with an air of mystery and humor, as she dragged boxes to the edge of the sand and seated herself on the warm grass. Several small, green grasshoppers leapt out of the way in a pretty panic.

Each carton was jammed full of old-fashioned, quart-size canning jars – clear, green, or palest blue – with matching lids, red gaskets, and heavy wire clamps that snapped with a resounding "click" over the tops. Sight of the jars flooded Augusta's mind with memories: Grandma canning peaches, Mother pressing apples through a cone-shaped sieve with a wooden pestle, the sweet, spicy aroma of cinnamon.

"Nowadays we do a lot of canning in Miraton," Andrea explained, "but I found these old jars in people's attics and garages. I just went around begging. Now, here's what we're going to do." And with that, she scooped a couple of handfuls of clean sand into a jar and thrust a candle into it, twisting it sharply to set it deep and upright. "Voila!"

Augusta was enchanted. The lights for the evening's gathering were windproof and sturdy, no dripping wax or danger of fire. Admiring the ingenious candle holder, she was struck by the full scope of its symbolic message. It evoked a simpler time, the reuse of resources, preservation of food, the independence and security of a kitchen garden -- in fact, the hard work and nurturing roles of women. Oh, yes, the flame itself represented one woman's spirit. Augusta shook her head in amazement. "Oh, It's so perfect!"

CRONE; A Meditation on Womanhood

The younger woman tossed her hair back over her shoulders and grinned. "I think so, too. Lots of great symbolism and heavy nostalgia, huh? I invented it myself." The two of them began digging happily in the sand pile. Three young girls materialized out of nowhere to help them, and the work went quickly. "How many do we have?" Augusta finally asked.

"Almost four hundred, at last count," Andrea answered. "Some will bring their own, and I have three people assigned just to add new candles whenever one gets low. Ninety will circle the pond like a birthday cake.!"

"Ooooh!" cried the girls in one high-pitched voice, eyes wide and excited. "Can we do that?"

"Of course you can!" Andrea exclaimed. "I'll trust you to count out exactly ninety – and spread them evenly all around the water's edge. Won't it look marvelous?" The girls bounced up and down with excitement, the littlest one clapping her hands and dancing a jubilant jig.

The adults lifted some of the now-much-heavier boxes into the cart, leaving the rest for a second trip, guiding the load back down the hill to the spring. "Let's start here," the director instructed her helpers. "Three on the top of the rocks," and she pointed to the flat outcropping. Judy, the oldest, climbed up with no difficulty and positioned the bottle-lamps, to be viewed, like a lighthouse beam, from the lower meadow. "I want to light these myself tonight," Judy stated resolutely.

"Then you shall," Andrea assured her. "First, we'll leave 150 by this rock, with extra candles and plenty of matches. People can pick them up and light them right here. Now, one every ten steps aaaaaall the way to the cottage," she said, pointing dramatically to the stone house nestled into the side of the hill.

The three little girls were in deadly earnest about their duty. Mary, with large dark eyes and strong legs, marched first up the hill, counting: "One... two... three... four..." extending each leg as far as it could reach, arms outstretched for balance. Jean, more reserved, walked behind her with a bottle, mindful that each unlit candle remain absolutely upright. At every count of "Ten!" she

CRONE; A Meditation on Womanhood

placed one in the grass exactly where Mary's toe pointed. Judy brought up the rear, doling out bottle lamps from the cart, and equalizing spaces a bit, when the younger girls weren't looking.

By the time the little work crew reached the pond, several women, traveling between camp and cottage, had praised the girls for their achievement. Augusta gave them a quick lesson in planning and math. Judy, who could count the highest, walked around the pond once, to determine the total number of steps, and they divided 472 by 89. The children never understood why they needed to subtract one. Five steps "and a little extra," worked out perfectly, and the gigantic birthday cake was soon complete, with ninety nicely spaced bottles. The white-goose decorations, swimming on the monster "cake," retreated angrily to the center island, where they spent the whole afternoon alternately dozing and complaining.

CHAPTER EIGHTEEN

Andrea and Augusta found Faith happily positioned by the kitchen door, snapping tips from the ends of crisp green beans, and dropping them into an old colander "Grandma and Mahm are taking a nap, she half-whispered, "but I can have lunch ready for you in a coupla minutes."

"Wonderful," Andrea retorted in an equally hushed tone, depositing several candle-lamps on the other bench. Augusta noticed that one candle-jar had already arrived before them. It was nestled among the red-stemmed vines that lined the cottage wall, and were fast spreading under and between the bench legs. The bottle looked just a little different, for some reason. Studying it more carefully, she noticed that rice was supporting the candle rather than sand.

CRONE; A Meditation on Womanhood

"What does the rice mean?" Augusta queried, knowing that little happened here by accident.

"Oh, rice is symbolic of so many things, you know ... life and fertility, self and abundance. In some cultures, each grain is believed to have a soul," Faith explained. "It's my birthday gift to Mahm." Augusta understood.

Suddenly she became very curious about two elderly women, who were comfortably seated with their backs against a large tree. Who are they?" she asked, gesturing toward them with a nod of her head.

"Oh, you mean Oofie and Doodle," Andrea replied with a grin, waving to them.

"Are they sisters then?" Augusta surmised because of the child-like names.

"Better than that. They knew each other before they were born."

Augusta was stymied for just an instant. "Ah, their mothers were friends, and were pregnant together!"

"Wow, you're good at riddles! Andrea said. "C'mon. We'll be right back." The two continued on up the back hill, leaving a trail of unlit luminaries along the path to the outhouse. "Have you made any decision?" Augusta asked, as they walked.

Andrea shook her head. "I'm not sure you'd call it a decision," she explained, "but I do have an appointment with a counselor this week. I want to take my time; study all my options."

"Well, that's great," Augusta commented. "Yesterday I thought you felt trapped into one particular action. Have you asked any of the women for ideas?"

"Yes, I've been doing that. In fact, Linda asked me to move in with her. She's willing to take care of the baby while I'm working and going to night school, if I can baby-sit for Jenny and pay room and board. It would be a good arrangement for both of us." She sighed deeply. "I'm looking at every side of it. But getting *really* responsible is tough!" Turning to head back down the hill, they both laughed at that comment, recognizing the hard truth of it. They knew a daily tug-of-war went on inside their heads –

CRONE; A Meditation on Womanhood

trying to make healthy decisions when easier answers always seemed to loom seductively before them.

On their return to the cottage, Faith and Maddie greeted them with a neat stack of whole wheat sandwiches – egg salad, cucumber, cream cheese and watercress (Augusta's favorite) – and a dessert basket of bananas, nectarines and grapes. An antique fruit knife with a carved silver handle lay invitingly, handle up, against the woven wicker side. The guests, far hungrier than they had realized, ate silently, joyfully.

Andrea, lifting up an old pitcher with worn, painted roses, offered to pour some iced tea. "Oh, wait!" Augusta said, pulling at the purple bandanna, and holding out her elegant mug with its peacock cottage design. She tucked the cloth back into her pocket, and took her first sip. The tea surprised her, with its aromatic hint of almond flavoring and mint sprigs. Faith said it was called "Tatnuck Punch," although she had no idea why.

"I think everything's pretty well organized for tonight," Faith reported. "Just remember to sign the ledger."

"Whoa! Thanks for reminding me," Andrea exclaimed. Now the only thing left is to set up the table for the cakes." She dragged two long, thick planks and two sawhorses, out from under the cottage stairs, and scrubbed the pieces down with soap and water. As they carried them to the springhouse, Faith explained that this makeshift banquet table had been assembled during the Crone's first summer here, and was traditionally placed right *here*, near the springhouse, so that a large crowd could be served without disturbing cook or kitchen.

"Twenty people have promised to bring their favorite carrot cake recipes, so I think we'll have enough," Andrea commented with satisfaction, as she spread open the newest ledger, and laid it lovingly on the boards, signing with a flourish under the three dozen or more signatures already penned by this morning's visitors.

Augusta signed next, startled by the voice just behind her that declared, " "Hey! It looks like we're having a party!" Augusta turned to greet a woman of her own age, with a family resemblance she'd come to know well in the features of Faith, and Leigh, and the Crone. "Faith's mother!" she blurted out.

"Oh yes, it's that obvious," Olivia replied, grinning, as she rested a battered guitar case against one of the sawhorses. "But I'm afraid no one ever mistakes us for twins! I'll bet you're the writer we've been expecting."

"Well," Augusta hesitated a moment, "I think I might be, at that. How did you know?"

"We put the message out there three days ago," she said cryptically, sending an uneasy shudder down Augusta's back.

"How so you mean that?" Augusta tried to sound nonchalant.

"Oh, nothing too crazy," Olivia replied with a chuckle. My mother and I meditated early one evening up at the Seat. Do you know where I mean?" Augusta nodded. "And we just mentioned our need to the Universe."

Augusta sighed. "Was it a beautiful sunset?" she asked.

"Indeed it was!" Olivia declared. I visualized a woman walking up the path to the cottage, traveling west."

"And that's the message I clearly received!" exclaimed Augusta in amazement. "I kept hearing, 'Go toward the sunset,' but I couldn't imagine what it meant."

"That's all right, then," Olivia replied with the Crone's same self-assured inflection. "Has my mother spoken about the project to you yet?"

"Oh, yes. Leigh and I had quite a long talk. It interests me very much. I'll do my best with it." Augusta answered fervently.

"Good. We'll get together over the next few weeks. Do you live close by?"

"Just over those mountains, about ten miles north of here," Augusta explained. "Easy trip."

Olivia picked up her guitar case, and the three women headed back to the cottage, pausing for a long moment to observe the growing tent and van population far below.

"I think we'll just sing a song, as everyone walks up the hill." Olivia was explaining. "The one that Mahm wrote a few years ago, called 'We are We.' We all know it. Then Leigh can give a short speech, we'll sing 'Happy Birthday,' and end with the Women's Credo. My mother says the cards are all printed. Oh heavens, when can we hand them out?"

"Leave that to me," Andrea replied. "I'll put some next to the Gift Ledger, and pass out the rest. I know three energetic girls who'll be glad to help." She and Augusta laughed at the allusion to the three candle-lamp distributors. "We're keeping it simple, and I'm sure it'll flow smoothly."

Suddenly Faith was swooping out of the cottage, running full tilt down the path toward them, Grumpkin close underfoot. She hugged her mother with little sounds of delight, and the two were soon wrapped up in mother-daughter talk.

Augusta, with underlying surges of puzzling emotion, drew away from the little group to observe their interaction. Something about the strength of these women—their open acceptance and vitality, their positive, no-nonsense outlook – was inspiring, even beyond the obvious love they shared. It affected everyone: Maddie was stronger already, was learning to reach out, and Augusta felt herself summoned to a new adventure. It was mystifying and marvelous.

The Crone, having come downstairs from her nap, was standing in the doorway of her stone cottage. She was only a small, spare, ancient woman, patiently waiting to welcome her granddaughter, but her dignified bearing gave her the majesty of a spiritual leader. Whatever charisma is, she has it, Augusta thought, and so do Leigh and Olivia and Faith. She was surprised to see how much Olivia, bending to kiss her grandmother, towered over her.

"Oh, let's have a picture of four generations," Andrea exclaimed, waving her camera, calling for a pose in front of the door. Leigh stepped out of the shadow of the cottage, tallest by far, her crown of whitening hair a dramatic halo around her face. She stood behind Olivia and Faith, putting her arms around their shoulders, and giving each a smile and a squeeze. Olivia and Faith stood almost shoulder to shoulder, their hands laid gently on the

CRONE; A Meditation on Womanhood

Crone's bony shoulders, as she positioned herself in the foreground. It was a curious pose, Augusta thought, because of the extreme differences in their heights.

Suddenly Faith called excitedly, Hi! Caroline! We're taking pictures – c'mon!" She broke away from the group, trotting down the hill toward a five year old girl, scooping into her arms a miniature copy of herself. Almost at once the child struggled to be put down. She ran to the trio of women at the door, stretching her arms out to them all equally, sure that she would be enveloped in the warmth of their love.

"Hello, I'm Sophie," announced the woman who had brought Caroline, coming up the hill to stand beside Augusta. She was a carbon copy of Olivia, but with darker coloring and deeper set eyes, the wrinkles of age only the faintest web-dusting across her face. She was plainly dressed in T-shirt and jeans, with a sweatshirt tied above her belt. Next to the ubiquitous mug, Augusta noticed a long, deerskin pouch hanging at her waist. It was the woman's only distinctive ornament, yet Augusta sensed some elusive, even other-worldly, quality about her.

Sophie surveyed the homestead, noting every well-remembered detail, shaking her head in amazement. "It's always more beautiful than I remember it. When I'm feeling pressured, I just recall this view, and relax instantly. Every time, it feels like I've come home again." She paused, savoring the pleasure of it. "Have you been down to 'tent city' today? There must be fifty campers, and more coming in every minute."

"Yes, I have. My name's Augusta by the way. This gathering has been a total surprise to me." The two chatted together like old friends, as they observed the taking of the historic five-generation photograph.

The Crone was allowed to settle on her bench at last, appearing to be at once flustered and pleased by all the family attention. "Much of a muchness," she muttered, only half in jest. "Where's Sophie?" The tone of her voice was close to a command, and the most recently arrived granddaughter ran forward eagerly.

CRONE; A Meditation on Womanhood

"Are you reading my stones today, Sophie? The ancient one questioned.

"Yes, of course, Mahm, I'd be honored," Sophie replied, unconsciously patting the deerskin pouch as she spoke. Intrigued, Augusta followed the stone-reader into the dark cottage, as several women came forward from the campground to wish the Crone well, and receive her blessing in return.

CHAPTER NINETEEN

A huge bowl of tossed salad and loaves of garlic bread were laid out on the table, next to a cruet of home-made French dressing. The aroma of spicy vegetable lasagna wafting from the oven gave the keeping room a festive air. "Would I be interrupting anything?" Augusta asked Sophie hesitantly.

"Not in the least – I'd love the company," Sophie answered her, as she moved the food from the table to the sink, and untied the deerskin pouch from her belt. Outside, Olivia was tuning her guitar, her little audience finding seats on the grass, and against the big rock, eager to hear her latest tune. "I've written music to Peacock Cottage," she was explaining. "It's got a kind of lullaby-dance rhythm, if that's possible," she laughed, "... and I think it is." Her fingers caressed the strings lightly, and she hummed as she wove the theme, building and broadening her harmonies. The music drifted through the doorway and open window, a fitting background to the stone-reader's work.

Seated at the table, Sophie began her ritual, first drawing an ancient, handmade lace square from the drawstring pouch, and spreading it out smoothly on the scrubbed wooden surface. Augusta sat opposite her, observing her actions with intense interest. Next, Sophie withdrew a smaller deerskin bag, tied with a double knot to preserve its precious contents.

"May I?" Augusta asked, reaching for the empty pouch. The stone-reader nodded absentmindedly. Augusta handled it reverently, pressing butter-soft, tanned and bleached deerskin, stitched with tight loops of leather thong in the Amerindian fashion. Darker, uncut edges fell away on one side in freely rippling forms; a single long strand was weighted with an African "third-eye" bead of blue and white glass. Two brown speckled wing-feathers from the homestead's peacocks hung from beaded thongs. "The pouch was a present from Mahm," Sophie explained.

A stream$^{\Omega}$ of semi-precious stones slid, with a tinkling chatter, from the smaller pouch into Sophie's left hand. Closing her right hand protectively over them, she repeated "Crone of the Mountain, my Mahm" several times in a soft whisper, then turned her hands in a praying gesture over the cloth, and let the contents fall. Perhaps twenty stones, each equally beautiful in its color and tumbled shine, scattered in an open pattern both on and off the lace, determining their relationships. Augusta was fascinated by the variety – sparkle of fool's gold, gleam of tiger's eye, luster of carnelian, glow of pink quartz. But what could they possibly reveal to the woman who was about to read them? Augusta's skepticism was terribly strong, but she hoped a little open-mindedness was available to her, too.

"This is a wonderful opportunity," Sophie explained, "but I wanted Mahm's approval first. A reading done without someone's express consent is the worst form of violation."

Augusta instantly vacated her seat at the table when the Crone came into the shadowed room. The ancient woman lowered

---

Ω When this book was written, Jean Brookwell cast a stone-reading, exactly as described here. Each of these 33 stones has a predetermined meaning (verified by the author). The reading is accurate. We were both astonished by this validation of the Crone's life and purpose. Layout sketch is on pages 116-117.

herself cautiously into the chair, and peered intently across the table at her granddaughter.

"Oh, how interesting!" Sophie exclaimed in a hushed voice. "The stones have landed in three sections. These on the cloth are your life and purpose, Mahm. And, over here ..." she indicated a scattering of stones off the lace, to the left, "your heritage," To the right, your legacy to the world. Notice," (Sophie included Augusta in her explanation), "there is great symmetry here."

"Oh, Mahm, how true this is! Look. The uppermost stone is *Love*; it confirms your life purpose." The Crone nodded contentedly, as Sophie turned to Augusta. "In this incarnation, she's achieved the ability to love her entire life -- all the difficult and fortunate events, all the people. She now sees every incident as totally without error." The stone-reader looked into the Crone's eyes and saw only serene affirmation.

"Notice here," Sophie went on, pointing to the two stones below *Love*. These are *Gift* and *Confusion*. Mahm's life work identifies confusion as a gift to be accepted joyfully. It's the first step toward personal growth. When a woman lets go of her passive up-bringing and reaches for her inherent power, confusion is the first experience, isn't it?" The women nodded. "Mahm works with this stone, called '*Understanding the Correct Use of the Body*', which is next to '*Happy Fault*'. You see, a woman all too often has difficulty understanding her body, seeing it as something to be bartered or, even worse, battered. But '*happy fault*' is just what the name implies. All faults exist for the purpose of teaching both the owner and the receiver – and what teaches can hardly be called *fault!* Notice the *Money* stone is near the center, but this little sharp pointer is directed toward her heritage. That means Mahm has always had enough money."

While listening to Sophie's explanation, Augusta had been intently studying the layout. Now she understood that each of these tiny gems had its own inherent meaning; the relationships were obvious to anyone who analyzed them. Despite her

CRONE: A Meditation on Womanhood

skepticism and doubt, the validity of the message itself caught at her imagination.

"Mahm originally acquired her sense of self here" (pointing to three stones in a tight cluster), "through her family and her second husband. He constantly belittled her, but, in her struggle not to accept his scorn as truth, she found her own magnitude. This is the *unanswered question* stone pertaining to that husband, and also to her father, who sexually abused her." Sophie was abruptly startled from her monologue. "Oh, Mahm, is that true? When I saw "negative outlook" next to the "father" stone, I suddenly felt sexual abuse. You never told me that."

The Crone nodded curtly, with a pinched look that Augusta interpreted as an expression of long-buried pain. It explained the vehemence of the old woman's attitude during the discussion of incest the previous evening.

"And here..."Sophie pointed to another small cluster, her voice acquiring a positive lilt, "we see that her body and spirit are in perfect harmony. You are content with both, aren't you, Mahm? The *Popeye* stone says so." And Sophie began to giggle, explaining to Augusta that a certain stone, whose meaning had at one time puzzled her, had finally revealed itself as "I yam what I yam."

Augusta was delighted with the interpretation.

"And that's all, Mahm, unless you want me to go on?"

The Crone looked into her eyes. "Beautiful!" she pronounced it. "I couldn't ask for more."

But Augusta, having noticed Sophie's shift in attitude, reached out and swiftly picked up the tiny piece of jet-black onyx. "What does this one mean?" she asked pointedly.

Sophie hastily gathered up the stones, and sent them chattering into the deerskin pouch. She avoided Augusta's eyes as she replied in a strained whisper, *"Negative outlook."*

CRONE; A Meditation on Womanhood

A Gathering of Women

CHAPTER TWENTY

The sun, sliding far behind the cottage, threw the first of the evening's long shadows across the path and meadow. Down on the campground, a couple of small fires became visible pinpoints of light in the gathering dusk. Caroline sat cross-legged on the floor, thrilled to the point of shaking – fearful of dropping the mewing little ball whose eyes were tight-closed, whose splayed feet had the merest pinprick of claws -- when Leigh laid the newborn kitten into her small cupped hands.

Faith and Maddie completed their preparations with singing and laughter – salad tossed, bread heated and sliced, tray of lasagna cut up in squares – and called the guests to supper. The little girl and eight women found seats on benches, chairs or grass and ate hungrily, happily, slipping tiny pieces of food to the begging dog and the more particular cats, all of whom had been well fed before supper.

The geese remained huddled on their island, squawking occasionally, imprisoned there by the presence of the crowd. At dusk, the peacocks and their hens rose into the trees with a whirring flap of wings, hopping to higher branches until they were settled thirty or forty feet above the ground in their nighttime perches.

Andrea's organizational mind continued to mull over the evening's simple plans. "Augusta, will you be responsible for the water pitcher? I'm leaving a couple of big candles in the springhouse, so you'll have no trouble seeing."

"Sure," Augusta answered. "Glad to help." Retying her precious mug to her waist, she wandered toward the garden for a panoramic view of her surroundings, and attempted to analyze her experiences of the past few days. It had been a kind of culture shock, this continuous feeling of acceptance and peace, much like an AA meeting, she thought – friendly, welcoming, safe.

What struck her most about the preparations for the Gathering was the tacit assumption that all would unfold exactly as it was meant to – an unspoken acknowledgment of the rightness of the outcome, planned for but not manipulated. This approach nurtured a serenity that was no mere attitude, but a deep, spiritual trust, a conviction, a certainty that spread like a protective umbrella over the homestead, and endowed the participants with a sense of meaning and mission. She knew that it resonated through the air, sang through the pines, and reverberated through the heart of every woman who had ever made a pilgrimage to the stone cottage. Augusta was beginning to recognize it as that rare blessing: Esse's unconditional love, translated into human terms.

* * *

Unbeknownst to her, the other women were illuminating the cottage. Sophie attended to every bottle-lamp along the path to the outhouse, including the big candle inside, while Leigh touched a match to the wicks of the two kerosene lamps, upstairs and down. Olivia laid a fire for later in the evening, when the cold air of the mountain night was certain to return. Maddie and Faith had polished up the kitchen, while Andrea gave everyone a little box of wooden matches and a couple of candles, to keep alive the enchanted, fairy quality of the approaching evening.

Augusta discovered the Crone already well ensconced on her bench, a soft pillow under her, a shawl around her, and a mug of herb tea beside her. "What more could I ask for?" she muttered, with the slightest undertone of sarcasm, unnoticed by her busy relatives, but silently noted by Augusta, who couldn't help thinking that being ninety was hardly unrelieved joy. Andrea lit a couple of lamps close to her feet, but the Crone waved them away. "Can't see," she said, signifying that they cast a blinding glare.

"Here they come! Here they come!" shouted Caroline, jumping up and down and pointing to the campground. Sure enough, the three bottle-lamps on the rocks above the spring had been lit. Augusta hoped that little Judy had gotten her wish.

The leader, Linda, was walking with slow and measured step up the meadow path toward the barn, followed every few feet by another woman or child, each carrying the glow of a bottle-protected flame. Augusta hurried down to her position in front of the springhouse, lighting her own lamp and those on the banquet boards. She gathered three pitchers in her hands and ran to the springhouse, where the two big candles inside were throwing long shadows along the rough rock wall. Quickly scooping water into the pitchers, she left one, and rushed two back to the table, not wanting to miss another moment of the ceremony.

The line of lights had not yet passed the barn, when suddenly three flames broke away and wobbled rapidly toward the pond. Augusta laughed; no question who they were: three little girls who would never forget this night!

Across the meadow now, faintly, unmistakably drifted the sound of many voices, singing. Although she couldn't yet make out the words, it was undoubtedly the Crone's song, a simple round very like "Row Your Boat," or "Frere Jacques." The chorus had a

CRONE; A Meditation on Womanhood

snappy, upbeat rhythm, while the verses wove a slower melody through the driving words of the refrain.

She strained to make out the message, when suddenly Olivia appeared strumming her guitar, and the lyrics took form at last:

> We are one with the sun
> And the wind and the sea;
> We are one – or we're none.
> We are one; we are we.

Some of the children put added emphasis on the last "we!" Olivia sang the first verse for her. It evoked the whole life of the Crone with its simplicity and truth:

> What I do touches you;
> What you do touches me.

And the refrain came through loud, clear, and compelling as the line of women halted, bunched together at the pond to watch the three girls moving purposely from year to candle-year.

> What I do changes you;
> What you do changes me.

And again, lightly syncopated, the refrain was carried by each chorus. What choir-mistress had stood at the spring to start each group on the first verse again? All was a marvelous bewilderment to the senses, a blend of intertwined voices and a blur of twinkling lights, magnified by curved bottle walls, as the miniature valley grew rapidly darker, and the sunset, awash with purple and gold, absorbed the light of the upper sky.

CRONE; A Meditation on Womanhood

So renew and redo;
Love anew is the key.

As the parade of women and children continued their pilgrimage toward the cottage, the sky darkened to pale gray-mauve velvet. In warm contrast, the kerosene lamps glowed ever brighter through the windows, a beacon to those climbing the hill. The procession approached its destination, laughing and singing, some of the young girls so in awe that they held tight to their mothers, while others skipped along at the edge of the throng, candles bobbing precariously. The crowd formed a great semicircle before the cottage, setting their candles on the ground to sing one last full round, clapping in time with the music: clap-clap-*clap*, clap-clap-CLAP – every third word a heavy beat:

We are ONE with the SUN
And the WIND and the SEA;
We are ONE – or we're NONE!
We are ONE; we are WE!

And the last word was a shouted WHEEE! that thrilled everyone, young and old alike, with its spontaneity. The Crone applauded vigorously from her throne, setting the crowd to still greater applause. A tight lump appeared unbidden in Augusta's throat; the crowd parted as if on cue, so that this honored lady might view her giant "birthday cake" – an uneven ring of ninety candles encircling the pond like tiny stars, glinting across the water, magnified and fragmented by the gentlest ripple.

This ancient, venerated woman raised her hands above her head and applauded, then clasped them together like a prizefighter. Someone blew an ear-piercing, two-fingered whistle. The throng roared, laughed, cheered – and then abruptly, unexpectedly, the audience hushed.

Olivia waited for a long moment before strumming one heavy chord on her guitar. She began to sing, "Happy birthday to

CRONE; A Meditation on Womanhood

you..." and the crowd joined with her, "happy birthday to you, happy birthday dear Mah-ahm, happy birthday to you." The Crone didn't attempt to stand, but raised her arms again, this time in benediction, nodding gratefully and gracefully.

Leigh stepped forward to stand beside her mother, her great height overshadowing the tiny woman, and the tenor of the crowd was instantly uneasy and remote. Reacting quickly to the sharp change in atmosphere, Leigh immediately stepped aside and down the hill, so that the crowd would hear her voice, but the lights and focus of attention would remain only on the person of the Crone. It was a fine, spontaneous piece of staging.

"Thank you all for coming," Leigh called out in her strong voice. "This is a magnificent tribute to a woman who has so powerfully touched our lives. She has given us music and poetry, and a philosophy to live by. But most of all, she has given us all ... her love. Tonight we return it to her tenfold!" (Scattered applause, increasing in volume and strength.)

"Let us conclude this gather of women by reading together the Credo that Mahm has written for us ... and for all women."

As if they were a superbly rehearsed Greek chorus, the women bent down for their lamps as with a single movement. The suddenly levitated lights threw haunting shadows on every face. Augusta dug in her pocket for her glasses. Tipping her card close to the bottled light, she read aloud in measured cadence with these women, who had gathered here tonight to celebrate one woman's life, but, in so doing, stayed to celebrate themselves.

CREDO

I am a woman, a spiritual being,
(they spoke in unison.)
One with Creation, and in rhythm with the moon.
(Their voices were vibrant.)
My life is a gift from Mother Earth;
Each day I replenish and care for Her,
Treating all life with reverence.
I am responsible for my every act,
For my body and mind are my own.
(Augusta felt the rising emotion in their voices,
matched by her own.)
I love each woman as myself,
And shield all children from harm.
(Yes, Augusta thought, this is a creed to live by.)
Devoted to my true potential,
I offer my talents to the world
in truth and harmony,
At one with the Will of he Universe.

A profound, passion-filled silence settled over the throng.
It was a hole in time, a frozen eternity -- a moment with no future
expectation. What could possibly follow this, Augusta wondered?
And then the answer came, faintly, softly at first, one voice and
then another. "Amen" was a fervent whisper that grew into a
floating, rippling crescendo: "AMEN!"

CRONE; A Meditation on Womanhood

CHAPTER TWENTY-ONE

Soft guitar music touched and then entered the silence gently, unobtrusively. It was Olivia strumming her newly composed lullaby-dance, "Peacock Cottage," the unspoken signal for the throng to break, ceremony completed. Again together, but oddly like a single woman, they bent over to place their lamps on the grass, and lined up for their slices of poppy seed cake, or squares of carrot cake, and spring-water -- and to greet the Crone – in little laughing clumps of two and three, their voices blending in perfect harmony with candle-gleam and melody and moist night air.

"Hi, isn't this marvelous?" exclaimed Linda, embracing the whole homestead with an all-inclusive sweep of her arms. She slid behind the banquet boards to serve the Crone's favorite carrot cake, chuckling as she noticed the absence of paper napkins and plates. "Leave it to Mahm not to waste a single tree. I guess our bandanas and mugs will get good use tonight!" With that comment, she leaned over to serve some little girls with wide, expectant eyes, their cupped hands eagerly stretched out to her. "Look at this, Augusta. Start them young. They know they can use their hands to save the world!"

Augusta's own hands were occupied, pouring cool spring water into proffered mugs, but the back of her mind registered that sentence: "*They know they can use their hands to save the world.*" How could she best describe the devotion and dedication of these women here at the Homestead? She knew this womanly power was concentrating elsewhere, in thousands of places, but her first assignment was to distill the atmosphere of this Gathering, to capture the essence of the Crone's simple vision. She shivered – how would she ever put into words the indescribable? – and laughed at her easy arrogance in believing that she could. But new insight gently corrected her. It wasn't arrogance. The Crone's family knew that they had called, and she had answered; without knowing why, she had been willing to venture forth. She could do

CRONE; A Meditation on Womanhood

it. Not if she worked hard enough, no. But if she let go and listened to life instead.

And suddenly it happened. Her scattered thoughts settled into a coherent message. The days she'd spent at the stone cottage – cooking, cleaning and caring – had taught her the lesson at last. Those things that women were willing and able to do, those mundane actions repeated again and again, were the skills Mother Earth required, and in fact needed desperately.

In Augusta's creative mind, "cooking" grew to mean replanting the lost vegetable garden, the vegetation that was the planet; "cleaning" meant rejecting the dirty energy of fossil fuels, to scrub the atmosphere with wind and sun power instead; "caring" was the willingness to pay attention, to make those things happen that *must* happen, with respect for our planet, and love for each other and for all things. What had Faith and Augusta said to each other? "It fills me with joy to see some defeated person come alive, and blossom with new hope."

Augusta was thinking: oh, the simplicity! Replenish; Repower; Rejoice! And women's global thinking, so often denigrated by men for it's feminine softness, for its "unrealistic" expectations, that didn't see so much the differences but the similarities – that did not expect war, but agreement. *Our* way of thinking, *our* way of being, will reach its ultimate purpose in the healing of the Earth.

The Crone's voice spoke clearly in her head, affirming her vision: "Yes, it will."

*C*HAPTER TWENTY-TWO

Everyone was quickly served -- water in mugs, small squares of cake in bandanas. It was not a meal, but more like a sacrament. (Augusta dropped that little thought into her mind as well.) Almost immediately the mothers and grand-mothers, ancient ones hand in hand with the very young, took up their lights and strolled leisurely down the hill, vowing to remember the beauty of this evening forever.

Augusta headed for the yellow lights of the cottage, drinking in the cool mountain serenity, just as the whippoorwill called from the sentinel pine – not a mournful sound, but a joyful invitation to "Come up here." Augusta thought she might indeed join Faith and Maddie and the other women for the night at the Seat, since Leigh would expect to make use of the second bed in the tiny cottage. She recalled seeing extra sleeping bags tucked under the stairs.

The Crone was alone at last, her head bowed, hands open on her lap, ready to receive whatever might be offered her. The lamps on either side of her glimmered with air-starved flames, on candle-stumps that need not be replenished.

Just as Augusta reached the big rock, Leigh touched her mother's shoulder. "Mahm?" She waited, then reached out once more. "Mahm!" The little group of women spun around at the sharp note of anxiety in her voice. Leigh bent over her mother for a long moment, sheltering her from the eyes of friends and family. At last she faced them, tall and commanding, a long sigh escaping from the depth of her heart.

"My mother has left us," she said.

CHAPTER TWENTY-THREE

Silence. Shock. Sharp, gasping intake of breath. No! It can't be! No! Not now! All the common words of denial erupted spontaneously from her family and friends. It's not possible, Augusta protested silently, feeling the slow-motion helplessness of a nightmare. I *know* she was alive just before the whippoorwill called! Olivia and Sophie reached instinctively for their mother, circling her with their arms; Maddie and Andrea, dazed and confused, leaned against each other. Faith swept her bewildered daughter high into her arms, pressing her own face into the little girl's chest, holding her breath.

"Mommy! Mommy! What's the matter?" Caroline cried, tugging at her mother's hair, pulling Faith's face upward toward her own. "Our Mahm has died, honey. Her spirit has gone away," she answered at last, with a long-drawn, choking sigh, hugging her little girl tightly to herself. "No, no, Mommy. There she is." The child pointed blithely to the corner of the cottage, a distance from the bench. Then, as they watched, she grinned and held her hand up, fingers rhythmically forming a waving motion one after the other, as if she were mimicking the gesture of someone she obviously knew well. "Oh, thank you, lamb," Faith exclaimed, still seeing no one, and beginning to cry openly.

The child's innocent behavior brought the women into action. Leigh took charge. "Tell everyone they can come back again now – to say good-bye. We're having Mahm's vigil and viewing tonight." Leigh spoke with authority. "And ask one of the villager's to tell Faith's husband immediately, and ask him to inform the rest of the family."

She gave directions that were instantly accomplished: Andrea to fetch a blanket, Sophie to light a fire, Augusta to heat a kettle, Maddie to replace candles, and Olivia to inform the last of the women who were still meandering toward the campground, candle-lights in hand.

CRONE; A Meditation on Womanhood

Olivia's flashlight searched the path ahead, as she trotted cautiously down the hill toward the receding candlelight . Almost immediately, she came upon Linda and two of her neighbors from Miraton. She spoke with them for several minutes, even re-counting Caroline's innocent gesture. Had she truly seen the Crone's spirit?

"So call me Cassandra," the last woman in line said with a sigh, alluding to the ancient oracle who always bore bad news. Soon the news was racing across the meadow, creating waves of shock and denial. The first breaker crashed over the campground "Oh, Esse, no! The Crone of the Mountain is dead!" The undertow of lament instantly erased the evening's euphoria. But the message was transforming as it swept on. The swell of a more powerful emotion surged forward, as a new wave always curls toward the shore: "She saved my life," "She trusted me to make the right decision," "She taught me so much," "Her spirit is in my heart," "Yes, her spirit will live forever."

*   *   *

Olivia and Linda returned to the cottage to find six women being instructed in the proper use of a blanket as a makeshift stretcher. Six pairs of hands firmly gripped the rolled edges of the blanket, pulled it taut, and lifted the Crone's body on Andrea's sharp "Now!" It was a light burden, and the small procession quickly reached the Dutch door of the bedroom, supported in front and behind by Leigh and Augusta as acolytes. Soon their cherished Mahm was laid gently on her bed, her own rice-filled candle-lamp brought glimmering to the bedside table.

The younger women collected every available candle, distributing them about the bedroom on windowsills and chest, table and armoire, until the room shimmered with shifting shadows and haloed points of light. Caroline, least distressed of the mourners, oohed and clapped at the sight, but was soon fast

CRONE; A Meditation on Womanhood

asleep, tucked into Augusta's bed of the morning that now seemed another time and world away.

Each woman paid her respects in her own way, then withdrew to the keeping room, allowing Leigh some private time with herself, her thoughts and her mother. Grumpkin scrambled far under the bed, distraught. In the keeping room below, the rhythmic sound of Leigh's rocking chair on the single floorboards overhead sounded like distant thunder.

Olivia, shifting logs on the fire, threw a bright spray of sparks up the chimney. She and Sophie sat in the wing chairs that had been traditionally reserved for Leigh and the Crone, mindful of their rapidly shifting status in the family. "I wonder if Mother will be staying here now. " Sophie said softly as she stared into the flames, and sipped her mug of hot tea. She avoided asking aloud what was on her mind: a mundane question, even frivolous, but symbolic. Would Mahm's daughter electrify the cottage? Could they, in fact, accept all the changes in their family?

"Oh yes, I think so," Olivia replied, equally intent upon the flames, unwittingly answering Sophie's unspoken questions as well. "She and Mahm had talked about her death, and made plans for the cottage. In fact, the grave was dug over a year ago, under the sentinel pine. It's covered with boards and dirt right now. The village gave legal approval and everything."

Augusta, seated at the kitchen table with Linda, couldn't help overhearing. "At the Seat? What a marvelous place to be buried!"

"Yes, it is!" Olivia acknowledged. "And I get the feeling Mahm planned this whole evening, don't you?" The women made soft sounds of assent.

"All I know," Augusta commented, "is that she died just after the whippoorwill called – and it sounded as if it was urging her to go toward the sunset."

Faith, seated on one of the little footstools next to the fire, began to laugh and cry at the same time. "Isn't that just like her, dammit! Obvious symbolism to prove her point! I've always thought she and Esse were in cahoots!" With that half-angry, half-

CRONE; A Meditation on Womanhood

humorous observation, she hurried outside to view the serenity of moonlight and stars. In a few moments she popped her head inside. "They're on their way," she said. "Come see."

*   *   *

Light, the perennial sign of Spirit, had become the theme of the homestead. The moon gleamed yellow-white, stars were a dusting of minute sparkles across the night sky, and every bottle-lamp around the pond had been restocked and re-lit. It was a fantasy of light - far more spectacular than the early-evening birthday – as the parade of candles once again snaked its way toward the cottage, this time through a moon-washed, warm-black night.

"What are they singing?" Augusta asked. The melody was a sad, lilting lullaby that permeated the air, and warmed itself around the hearts of its listeners.

"A song Mahm wrote in the seventies," Olivia explained. I composed the music. It's called 'Cradle in the Sky.' Every kid in Miraton knows it. Hold on. I'll get you the words." She returned with a fresh piece of paper . "We have lots. Keep it."

Augusta held the sheet close to her candle, to follow along with the approaching chant. Despite its somber purpose, several guitars in the procession added substance and weight to the music, and a festive, summer-party air to the evening:

> We hear our mother crying;
> With her winds we hear her cry.
> We hear our mother sighing;
> With her trees we hear her sigh.
> We hear our mother calling;
> With her rivers she is calling,
> To pray that we dare to change how we care;

CRONE; A Meditation on Womanhood

Replenish and share --
Or she will surely die.

We hear her creatures crying;
From the ocean deep they cry.
We hear her creatures sighing;
From the forests how they sigh.
We hear her creatures calling,
From the wetlands they are calling,
To pray that we dare to change how we care,
Replenish and share --
Or they will surely die.

Suddenly the meaning of the words struck her heart, and a flood of totally unexpected tears engulfed her – triggered in part by the loss of the Crone, yes, but also fueled by old, buried anguish.

We are her children crying;
You can hear us as we cry.
We are her children starving;
In the wasteland hear us sigh.
We are her children calling;
From the deserts we are calling,
To show that we dare to change how we care,
Replenish and share –
Or we will surely die.

Augusta knew they were tears for a whole lifetime of losses, sadnesses and regrets; for things said and (sadder still) unsaid, for lost youth and lost loves, destruction of the planet, imminent old age, poverty and pain – and yes, for her own eventual, inevitable release from this life she held so dear.

We are her children raging;
We demand much more than "try."
We are her children raging,

CRONE; A Meditation on Womanhood

For we know we do or die.
We are her children marching;
Through our cities we are marching,
To prove that we dare to show how we care,
Replenish and share –
Or Earth will surely die.

Andrea directed the procession around to the back of the cottage, to the open Dutch door. Augusta, following close behind the leader, was initially blinded by the dazzling flames. She stepped out of the mourners' line into the corner, instinctively separating herself from the moving throng to observe it. Just then, several people, already gathered around the Crone's bed, began the final verse:

We are her children vowing
Not to burn her to the sky;
We are her children knowing
Only greed will let her die.
Now her children are uniting,
Yes, the whole wide world uniting,
To know that we dare to change how we care,
Replenish and share –
Our cradle in the sky.

The last line drove a vision of her own babies and their long-gone childhoods into Augusta's already burdened heart. Then the procession hushed, and, for a long moment, their shuffling footsteps were the only sound she heard.

She was fascinated by the recurring rhythm of the ritual. As she watched, each mourner in her own way offered comfort to Leigh, and in turn was consoled by her. She greeted each woman by name, hugged her with compassion, or ministered to her helplessness. Augusta appreciated that it was a hard duty, but the Crone had prepared well for her own death. Each woman and child was handed a personal note, from a pile on the bedside table

CRONE: A Meditation on Womanhood

– an ivory envelope with her own name spelled out in the Crone's distinctive script. Then Leigh escorted each mourner to the stairs, a gesture mindful of her function as the Crone's daughter and hostess of the cottage.

Reassured by the gentle hum of many whispers, Augusta stepped back into line, pausing just for a moment before the Crone's bed. She looked at the composed, wrinkled face she'd grown to love in these past few days, and felt Leigh's presence beside her. "I know my tears aren't really for your mother," Augusta found herself saying. "They're for me. Each year, I seem to carry more memories and losses to every funeral."

Leigh hugged her hard. "Each death becomes every death." she said softly, handing the younger woman her own ivory envelope.

What had happened just then? Something in the incisiveness of that statement prompted Augusta to search the older woman's face intently, suspiciously, half-expecting to find the loquacious Leigh departed in this last hour and the Crone miraculously resurrected. No, it was only Leigh's gaze that met her own, but with perhaps a touch of the Crone's deep peace around her eyes.

The guest walked slowly and thoughtfully down the stairs to the keeping room, surprised to find it not crowded. Sophie and Olivia were talking with some of the guests from the comfort of the two wing chairs, but most of the women had already said their farewells, and taken the path down the hill toward home.

Augusta added a log to the fire, settled herself on one of the stools, and leaned against the warm stone, allowing her sorrow to dissolve into serenity, for this room was vibrant with memories of welcome, and the hearth, the very heart of the cottage, was ablaze with far more than firewood.

* * *

CRONE; A Meditation on Womanhood

$\mathscr{A}$FTERWARD

Augusta woke in her own bed, her room pale with the gray light of early dawn – or was it perhaps late dusk? Confused and disoriented, she drew deep breaths to clear her head. The fog slowly drifted from her mind, until she recalled that Linda had dropped her off at her own car, parked for three days undisturbed on the country road. Ah, then it must be early evening! She remembered coming home in a daze and crawling immediately into bed, exhausted by the events of the last few days and the stress of this most recent, sleepless night.

The time at the Crone's cottage was no dream. On the contrary, it seemed to be the most authentic experience of Augusta's life. She could still see the vigil: women whispering, crying – napping when they could, where they could, up at the mountain Seat, in wing chairs, propped against walls. No one thought to disturb the peacefully sleeping Caroline.

Before dawn, everyone gathered at the front door to welcome the summer solstice, the Bantam cock crowing in anticipation of first light. The sky turning palest gray, then pewter-yellow, and finally a conventional pink, as the sun rose above the mountain gracefully, rapidly, without clouds or fanfare. Chilled by the remaining night air, the little band bowed their heads, as Caroline enthusiastically urged them to "listen to life, like Mahm said." Far below, on the meadow, a couple of hundred villagers greeted the day with reverence and hope.

* * *

Augusta made a pot of strong coffee, surprised that she hadn't suffered caffeine withdrawal at the Crone's homestead. As it perked, the inviting aroma drifted through her bed-sitting room. She cleared papers from her desk, and clicked on the computer, her eyes resting on Leigh's manila envelope. Beside it sat Augusta's own bottle-lamp, the candle stump a congealed puddle on the sand, blackened wick marking center of the hard wax blob. Next to it was her cottage mug, peacock tail encircling the base, purple batik bandana streaked with crumbs of carrot cake and frosting.

A painful lump rose into her throat. Pouring coffee into the handleless mug, she held it gingerly near the rim with both hands and sipped cautiously, hoping to swallow the sadness. It would not leave her. For several minutes she perused Leigh's workshop outline, squinting, without the benefit of her reading glasses. It was a comprehensive plan for teaching women their new roles in the twenty-first century, promising purpose and continuity to any group of women involved in the total program. Indeed, the Crone had well understood that education is not enough. Touching another's spirit, *that* is her message, Augusta realized, having listened to so many women at the vigil. They all spoke of the Crone with such gratitude, and the word that recurred – no, resounded – throughout their remarks was "Empowering."

As a writer, she knew she was touching the core of the subject, but how to express the inexpressible? Aha, that was another problem entirely! She simply didn't have the writing skills for such a demanding yet delicate job, because the character of the Crone was both clear and elusive. Perhaps analyzing how the old woman had effected *her* might stimulate some inner resolution. She cast her mind back over the experiences of the past few days, and began to tick off the Crone's most powerful characteristics: she had been unconditionally accepting, for one. Oh, and she listened wonderfully well. (Augusta suspected the older woman hadn't spoken a thousand words in her presence.) She clarified truth, yes, and required personal responsibility; she expected simple honesty rather than perfection. More than that, she had created an atmosphere of trust, and made Augusta feel important from the moment they met. It had been an amazing feat, and she still didn't quite understand how it had happened.

Reaching for her glasses in the pocket of her grimy denim skirt, she felt the sharp corner of an envelope. Her name, *Augusta*, in that well-remembered thin handwriting, brought prickling tears to her eyes. Inside, only two short lines:

> Use your talents for all of us,
> with the blessings of Esse.
>
> *Augusta*

Her hands shook. The Crone's name was her own! Damn the coincidence! Talk about symbolism! Would she herself become a crone one day? She wanted desperately to avoid that question – it certainly warranted no further reflection today – but Augusta knew that her own approaching old age had been in the back of her mind for some time, unbidden, but certainly unbanished.

And she had not planned to become a part of this woman's movement to save Mother Earth. No. Leave it to more dedicated people. Younger people. But it seemed that Augusta had been chosen, and had clearly accepted the challenge. There was no going back. She fingered the Crone's Credo, the crisp card designed by Leigh, found herself reading aloud, "I am a woman, a spiritual being..." Idly turning the card over, she stared at a close-up photograph of the symbolic candle-lamp: single flame, single spirit. Leigh was no slouch at marketing, Augusta said to herself,

CRONE; A Meditation on Womanhood

with a sudden laugh. 'Replenish, repower, rejoice' was a gentle drumming in her mind.

But her brain was still a blank. She stared at her computer screen, at last forcing herself to begin typing -- an outline? a few words? – knowing that something, *anything*, might break the block that filled her head like soggy cotton batting.

"The women of Miraton are on the move," she typed, staring at it with an objective eye. Bullshit! Augusta hit the backspace hard. Not more heartless, "objective" reporting! Not this time!

"This is the decade of spirituality," she began again. True enough, she thought, reactivating backspace, but truth can be trite. She closed her eyes to meditate – to listen to life and love. "Esse, guide me. Thank you," she spoke in her silent, inner mind. Several minutes passed in an instant. Her own rather scruffy orange cat, Punkin, hopped onto her lap, shoving his head insistently under her arm, meowing hopefully. How he loved being involved in her writing. It was difficult to type with his head in the way, but she hadn't the heart to move him when he was purring so contentedly. Now she was intensely aware of the quiet hum of the computer's fan. The muffled tick of her fingers on the keyboard, the words as they appeared magically on the pale screen:

Chapter One

"What am I doing, in the midst of a mountain meadow, heaven knows where. . . ?" Augusta was thinking as she balanced precariously

✳   ✳   ✳

CRONE; A Meditation on Womanhood

CRONE; A Meditation on Womanhood

CREDO

AM A WOMAN,
A SPIRITUAL BEING,
ONE WITH CREATION, AND
IN RHYTHM WITH THE MOON.
MY LIFE IS A GIFT FROM MOTHER EARTH
EACH DAY I REPLENISH AND CARE FOR HER,
TREATING ALL LIFE WITH REVERENCE.
I AM RESPONSIBLE FOR MY EVERY ACT,
FOR MY BODY AND MIND ARE MY OWN.
I LOVE EACH WOMAN AS MYSELF,
AND SHIELD ALL CHILDREN FROM HARM.
DEVOTED TO MY TRUE POTENTIAL,
I OFFER M TALENTS TO THE WORLD
IN TRUTH AND HARMONY,
AT ONE WITH THE WILL
OF THE UNIVERSE.

MIRA LEIGHTON
1993

* * *

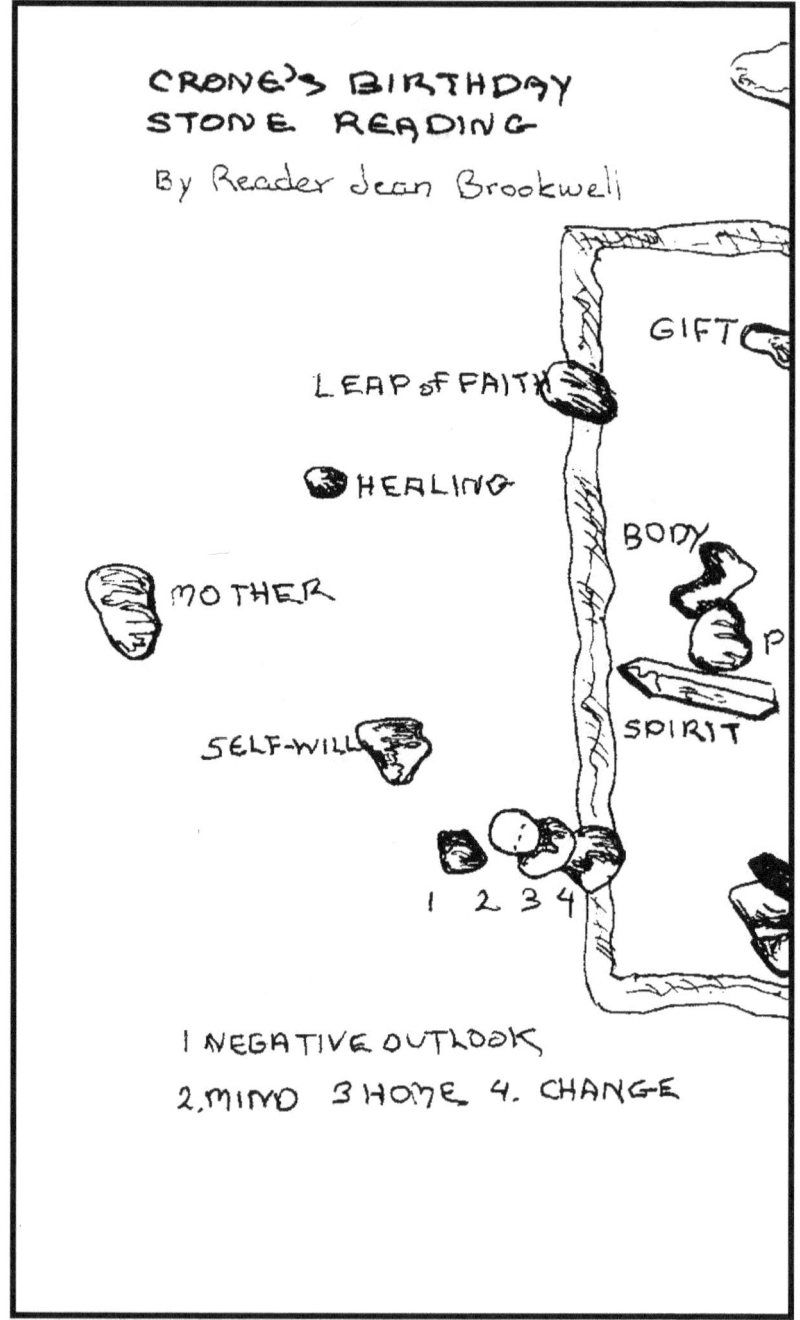

CRONE'S BIRTHDAY STONE READING

By Reader Jean Brookwell

GIFT

LEAP of FAITH

HEALING

MOTHER

BODY

P

SELF-WILL

SPIRIT

1 2 3 4

1 NEGATIVE OUTLOOK
2. MIND 3 HOME 4. CHANGE

CRONE; A Meditation on Womanhood

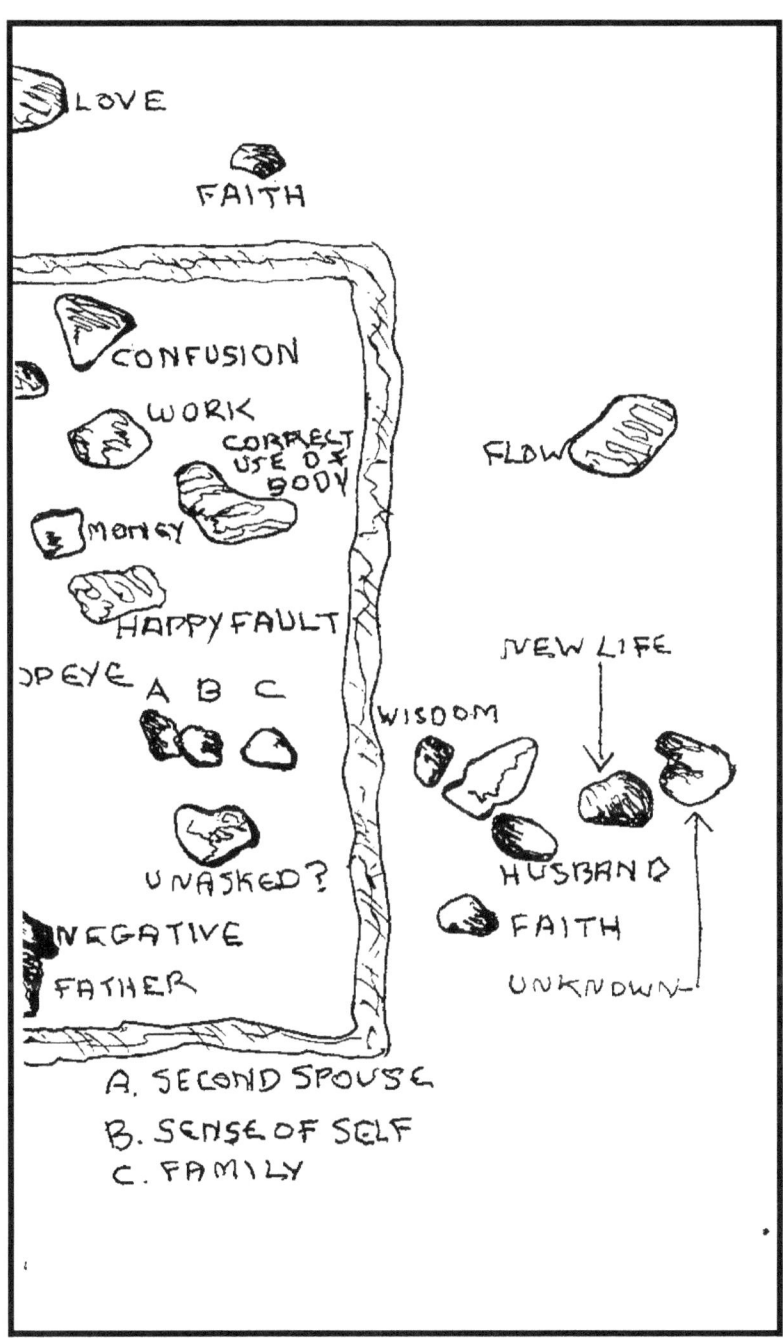

CRONE; A Meditation on Womanhood

CRONE; A Meditation on Womanhood

$\mathscr{G}$ATHERING OF WOMEN
Outline of a Proposal for a Series Of 12
Educational and Experiential Workshops

PURPOSE
To acknowledge and reinforce women as members of a self-responsible Sisterhood who, separately and collectively, aim to reach their full potential, employing all their talents for the good of Womanhood, and to protect and heal our Mother Earth.

1. I AM A WOMAN
- Women's historical and social contributions.
- Group techniques designed to promote interpersonal cohesiveness and self-esteem.

2. A SPIRITUAL BEING, ONE WITH CREATION
- To increase awareness of woman's place in religious history.
- Experiential workshops in meditation and yoga.

3. IN RHYTHM WITH THE MOON
- All aspects of women's health, including birth control, PMS, pregnancy, childbirth, menopause, cancers, and sexually transmitted diseases and AIDS.
- Prevention and management of women's diseases.

4. MY LIFE IS A GIFT FROM MOTHER EARTH
- Self-care, nutrition, disease prevention, positive life-styles.
- Dealing with the physical, mental and spiritual aging process.

CRONE; A Meditation on Womanhood

5. EACH DAY I REPLENISH AND CARE FOR HER

- Environmental issues, emphasizing personal action, purchasing power, lifestyle choices, and women's unique responsibility to reverse the population explosion.

6. TREATING ALL LIFE WITH REVERENCE

- The advantages of a vegetarian lifestyle to a woman's health, and as the appropriate use of limited planetary resources.
- Animal rights information.

7. I AM RESPONSIBLE FOR MY EVERY ACT

- Lectures, discussion and group process on self-responsible living and decision-making.
- Assertiveness training, undoing the "nice-girl" trap.
- Setting boundaries and saying "no."

8. MY BODY AND MIND ARE MY OWN

- Lectures and discussion on abuse, battering, rape, and harassment, and their prevention, management and recovery . Avoiding unwanted pregnancy, STDs and AIDS.

9. I LOVE EACH WOMAN AS MYSELF

- Education and groups on shared needs across generations.
- Setting up local and specific self-help groups.
- Group process on co-dependency and addictions.
- Supporting women with alternative life-styles, such as Lesbians and those in male-dominated professions.

10. I SHIELD ALL CHILDREN FROM HARM

- Education and discussion on child abuse and incest –
    prevention, responsibility, legal rights and recovery.
- A separate series of workshops on primary parenting for
    young mothers.
- Impact of media violence on young minds.

11. DEVOTED TO MY TRUE POTENTIAL

- Education and groups on self-esteem and risk-taking (such as
    ropes course and wilderness programs, and starting new
    business)
- Self-care as a basic philosophy.
- Discovering and nurturing talents and skills.
- Seeking further training and education.

12. I OFFER MY TALENTS TO THE WORLD IN TRUTH AND HARMONY, AT ONE WITH THE WILL OF THE UNIVERSE.

- Networking with women's groups
- Political activism
- Fully recognizing that men are not adversaries, but partners in
    service to humanity
- Choosing professions and programs that support women,
    children, and all humankind, for the health of the planet
    and world peace.

Replenish -- Repower -- Rejoice

XXX

CRONE; A Meditation on Womanhood

CRONE; A Meditation on Womanhood

THE *Peacock Cottage*

When I was a young girl, an innocent child,
I dreamed all those good days away,
With visions of gleaming white horses,
And a prince who would take me to stay
In a castle surrounded by peacocks,
Their tails fanned in gaudy display.

All too soon I became a young mother,
And I dreamed all those good days away
With visions of three perfect children
And a time when we'd all go to stay
In a castle surrounded by peacocks,
Their tails fanned in gaudy display.

Then my children grew up and they left me,
For dreams of their own far away,
With visions of three perfect households,
Yes, a time when they'd all go to stay
In their castles surrounded by peacocks,
Their tails fanned in gaudy display

Now I'm older and wiser by far,
I don't dream these good days away;
My children have children have children,
Now with grandma they sometimes will stay,
In my cottage – surrounded by peacocks –
Their tails fanned in gaudy display.

* * *

CRONE; A Meditation on Womanhood

*W*E ARE ONE

Refrain:
>   We are one with the sun
>   And the wind and the sea;
>   We are one – or we're none.
>   We are one; we are we.
>
>   What I do touches you;
>   What you do touches me.
>   Refrain
>
>   What I do changes you;
>   What you do changes me.
>   Refrain
>
>   So renew and redo;
>   Love anew is the key.
>   Refrain

(With syncopated beat:)
>   We are *One* with the *Sun*
>   And the *Wind* and the *Sea*;
>   We are *One* – or we're *None*!
>   We are *One*; we are *We*!

*   *   *

CRONE; A Meditation on Womanhood

CRADLE IN THE SKY

We hear our mother crying;
With her winds we hear her cry.
We hear our mother sighing;
With her trees we hear her sigh.
We hear our mother calling;
With her rivers she is calling,
To pray that we dare to change how we care;
Replenish and share --
Or she will surely die.

We hear her creatures crying;
From the ocean deep they cry.
We hear her creature sighing;
From the forests how they sigh.
We hear her creatures calling,
From the wetlands they are calling,
To pray that we dare to change how we care,
Replenish and share --
Or they will surely die.

We are her children crying;
You can hear us as we cry.
We are her children starving;
In the wasteland hear us sigh.
We are her children calling;
From the deserts we are calling,
To show that we dare to change how we care,
Replenish and share --
Or we will surely die.

CRONE; A Meditation on Womanhood

We are her children raging;
We demand much more than "try."
We are her children raging,
For we know we do or die.
We are her children marching;
Through our cities we are marching,
To prove that we dare to show how we care,
Replenish and share –
Or Earth will surely die.

We are her children vowing
Not to burn her to the sky;
We are her children knowing
Only greed will let her die.
Now her children are uniting,
Yes, the whole wide world uniting,
To know that we dare to change how we care,
Replenish and share –
Our cradle in the sky.

CRONE; A Meditation on Womanhood

PETERS VALLEY POPPY SEED CAKE

I was given this recipe while learning weaving techniques, 35 years ago, at Peter's Valley Craft Center, in New Jersey. This charming, historic village is filled with artists, and summer classes in many mediums such as blacksmithing, ceramics, weaving and jewelry.   Check out: www.pvcrafts.org

Pre-heat oven to 350º
4 eggs
3 cups flour
2 cups sugar
1 cup oil (like safflower)
1 teaspoon vanilla
½ teaspoon salt
1½ teaspoons baking soda
13 ounces evaporated milk

A 12 ounce can of poppy-seed filling
1 cup chopped nuts (optional)

First mix all ingredients together, except for the seeds and nuts.
Add seed filling. Beat at medium speed for 2 minutes.
Add chopped nuts

Pour into ungreased tube pan.
Bake for 70 minutes
Cool before removing from the pan.

Serve plain. Don't gild the lily!

CRONE; A Meditation on Womanhood

ℐCING for CARROT CAKE
Contributed by Lori Gordon

Suggestion
You may prepare this the day before it is needed, and chill overnight. The additional time improves the texture.

Ingredients
½ cup raw cashew pieces (optional; the texture is less like an
    icing and more like a pudding without cashews)
¼ pound tofu drained well (approximately 1 cup mashed)
½ cup real maple syrup
1 tablespoon vanilla extract
2 teaspoons almond extract
1 teaspoon orange extract

Directions
• Put cashews in food processor or blender; grind to a fine powder
• With blender or processor running, slowly add tofu, then syrup
    and flavorings. Beat until very smooth.
• Refrigerate a few hours or overnight before using.
• Whiz again briefly in blender or processor just before icing the cake (Make a layer cake of the two 8-inch rounds.)

*   *   *

FAVORITE CARROT CAKE
Contributed by Lori Gordon

INGREDIENTS
1 and ¼ cup real maple syrup
¾ cup canola oil
2 teaspoons. Vanilla extract
4 eggs
2 teaspoons Baking soda
2 teaspoons Baking powder
½ teaspoon salt
3 teaspoons cinnamon
1 cup whole wheat flour
1 cup unbleached white flour
2 ounces shredded dry coconut
½ cup finely chopped walnuts
3 cups shredded rap carrots, loosely packed
        (Shred by hand or food processor)

DIRECTIONS
- Pre-heat oven to 350 degrees
- Combine syrup, oil, vanilla, and eggs in large bowl. Beat until well-blended.
- Combine dry ingredients (except carrots) in another bowl, then combine with syrup/oil mixture
- Fold in carrots and stir until well-blended.
- Pour into 2 8" round pans, or one 11"X 14" pan, or, an 8-cup Bundt pan, or make 24 cupcakes.
- BAKE for 40 minutes (30 minutes for cupcakes) or until a toothpick inserted in the center comes out clean.

CRONE; A Meditation on Womanhood

$\mathscr{M}$IRA $\mathscr{L}$EIGHTON
(Judith M. Knowlton)

The author was born in Morristown, New Jersey in 1935. She is a graduate of Oberlin College, and was a Certified Addictions Counselor in New Jersey and Pennsylvania for 21 years.

Judy is the mother of three grown children: Garry, Howard, and Caroline. Their names became several characters in this book: Augusta (Garry's middle name is Augustus) And Leigh (Howard's middle name is Leighton). The names also acknowledge grand-children Jenny, Maddie, Olivia, Sophie, and Andrea (For grandson Andrew) and Jon, in memory of Jonathan.

She has written several books on addictions and personal growth and is the owner of QUOTIDIAN PUBLISHERS - which means "One day at a time" in Latin.

A widow, and now retired, she and her two cats make their home in the town of Cushing, in mid-coast Maine.

CRONE; A Meditation on Womanhood